THE GIRL'S BOOK OF
POSITIVE
QUOTATIONS

THE GIRL'S BOOK OF POSITIVE QUOTATIONS

Steve Deger and Leslie Ann Gibson

Fairview Press
Minneapolis

Dedicated to our "Littles"—
and the lessons *they* have taught *us*

Published by Fairview Press, 2450 Riverside Avenue, Minneapolis, MN 55454. For a free catalog of Fairview Press titles, call toll-free 1-800-544-8207, or visit our website at www.fairviewpress.org.

Fairview Press is a division of Fairview Health Services, a community-focused health system, affiliated with the University of Minnesota, providing a complete range of services, from the prevention of illness and injury to care for the most complex medical conditions.

Library of Congress Cataloging-in-Publication Data
The girl's book of positive quotations / [compiled by] Steve Deger and Leslie Ann Gibson.
　　p. cm.
　Includes index.
　ISBN 978-1-57749-175-0 (alk. paper)
1. Conduct of life—Quotations, maxims, etc.　2.　Success—Quotations, maxims, etc.　3. Motivation (Psychology)—Quotations, maxims, etc.
4. Women—Quotations.　I. Deger, Steve, 1966-　II. Gibson, Leslie Ann, 1956-
III. Title: Book of positive quotations.
　PN6084.C556G57 2008
　646.7--dc22

　　　　　　　　　　　　2008029137

Interior design: Ryan Huber Scheife, Mayfly Design (www.mayflydesign.net)
Cover design: Laurie Ingram

Printed in Canada
First printing: October 2008
12　11　10　09　08　　7　6　5　4　3　2　1

CONTENTS

Introduction

Have you ever had a girlfriend or an adult woman in your life who always seemed to know just the right thing to say—who offered the most encouraging words, right when you needed them the most?

Wouldn't it be great if she could always be there for you—not just a phone call or text message away, but actually right there in the room with you—offering a supportive hug when you were feeling down, or giving you a pat on the back whenever you did something well?

In this book, we give you not just *one* female friend like that but five hundred of them. Included here are wise, helpful, and inspirational insights from girls and women who have achieved fame and success in:

- Arts and entertainment
- Business
- Public service
- Science and exploration
- Sports

Each of them presents her life lessons within the pages of this book, for you to read and use when and if you need them. At some point in her life, each of these famous women has had to deal with the same issues you face in your own life: crummy moods, friendship and romance problems, personal challenges, self-doubt, and so on. And yet each has a found a way to rise above life's challenges and disappointments to find her own special place under the sun.

How (or *if*) you use this book is entirely up to you. You might skim through it, put it on your bookshelf, and not return to it for weeks, months, or even years. You might instead choose to keep it by your bed and pick a random quote to think about at the beginning or end of each day. Or you might just refer to it every now and then, when looking for a quotation to use in a presentation or report for a class at school.

Where, how, and *when* you find your inspiration are less important than that you do indeed *find* it, every day, throughout your life. If you don't find it in a book, look for it in the shining example of a family member, a teacher, a coach, or a member of the clergy. Or search for it deep within yourself, from that little voice inside you that knows more about you and your greatness than anyone else around you!

Chapter 1

WHAT MAKES YOU HAPPY?

Have you ever felt totally happy one minute, and then completely bummed out a few minutes later? Superhuge mood swings are normal for teen and preteen girls—they're part of the hormonal changes your body goes through before and after puberty.

Although you can't control your *feelings,* you need to make sure your *behavior* doesn't get out of control. Otherwise, you might say or do something really inappropriate—and end up in big trouble at home, at school, or with your friends!

Try the following tips when life has you feeling all weirded-out:

- Find a place and time to relax by yourself, away from whatever bugs you.

- If you get sad or angry with people, try not to yell or cry. Wait a few hours until you settle down, and then talk to them calmly about it.

- If you can't handle things by yourself, talk to a friend, a trusted adult, or a school counselor.

Finally, instead of dwelling on things that stress you out, why not make a list of the things that cheer you up and focus on those instead? Here is what some famous females put on their "happy lists." ✿

The thing that excites me isn't becoming a bigger star, but a better artist, deeper, truer to the things I find exciting.

— **JANET JACKSON**, SINGER, SONGWRITER, RECORD PRODUCER, DANCER, AND ACTOR

My mom, she is the most unbelievable mom that you could ever have in your entire life and she's always with me on everything. The most I've ever been away from her is two days. I love her more than anybody could ever know.

— **DAKOTA FANNING**, ACTOR

God will never give you anything you can't handle, so don't stress.

— **KELLY CLARKSON**, FIRST *AMERICAN IDOL* WINNER

I don't feel like I need a lot of things to make me happy.

— **HILARY SWANK**, ACTOR

I'm curvy—I'm never going to be 5'11" and 120 pounds. But I feel lucky to have what I've got.

—SCARLETT JOHANSSON, ACTOR

When I wake up in a bad mood, I try not to stay in one. Learn to make the best of what you have.

—FAITH HILL, COUNTRY SINGER

I just know rumors about me are going to keep coming, so I have to bear with it and not get too upset. You just have to ignore it sometimes.

—RIHANNA, BARBADIAN SINGER

If you aren't good at loving yourself, you will have a difficult time loving anyone, since you'll resent the time and energy you give another person that you aren't even giving to yourself.

—BARBARA DE ANGELIS, AUTHOR AND
    RELATIONSHIP EXPERT

We learn the inner secret of happiness when we learn to direct our inner drives, our interest, and our attention to something besides ourselves.

—ETHEL PERCY ANDRUS, FIRST FEMALE
   HIGH SCHOOL PRINCIPAL IN THE STATE OF
   CALIFORNIA

That is happiness: to be dissolved into something completely great.

—WILLA CATHER, AUTHOR

Paradise is exactly like where you are right now . . . only much, much better.

—LAURIE ANDERSON, PERFORMANCE ARTIST
   AND MUSICIAN

Whatever is—is best.

—ELLA WHEELER WILCOX, POET

Forget the past and live the present hour.

—SARAH KNOWLES BOLTON, WRITER

Life has got to be lived—that's all that there is to it.

—**ELEANOR ROOSEVELT,** FORMER FIRST LADY
AND CIVIL RIGHTS ACTIVIST

Think of all the beauty that's still left in and around
you and be happy!

—**ANNE FRANK,** GERMAN-BORN DIARIST AND
HOLOCAUST VICTIM

Love is like a beautiful flower which I may not touch,
but whose fragrance makes the garden a place of
delight just the same.

—**HELEN KELLER,** THE FIRST DEAFBLIND
PERSON TO GRADUATE FROM COLLEGE

We are new every day.

—**IRENE CLAREMONT DE CASTILLEJO,**
PSYCHOLOGIST

I have always felt that the moment when first you
wake up in the morning is the most wonderful of the
twenty-four hours.

—**MONICA BALDWIN,** AUTHOR

Sweets are good for the nerves.

>—**MARGARETE BIEBER,** ARCHAEOLOGIST
>AND ART HISTORIAN

Life is about enjoying yourself and having a good time.

>—**CHER,** SINGER AND ACTOR

Put a little fun into your life. Try dancing.

>—**KATHRYN MURRAY,** DANCER

Chapter 2

GET REAL!

Although it's important to set your goals high, it's also important to have realistic expectations for yourself and for others. You can't always get what you want, win every competition, or be the prettiest, smartest, or most popular girl in the world. And even if they try, your friends and family may not always know to be there for you when you need them.

Here are some tips to help you "get real":

- Practical goals involve practical steps. For example, it's realistic to expect to do well on a test at school—but only if you study, do your homework, and prepare *well in advance*. It's not realistic to think you can just cram the night before a test.

- Realize that things aren't always what they seem. Those photos of beautiful and skinny models in magazines have probably been airbrushed (or Photoshopped!). And all those "friends" who hang around the most popular girl in school might only be trying to look popular, too—they may not really care about her.

- Instead of expecting your friends and family to read your mind, make sure you *tell them* about your concerns and needs. You can't just assume they somehow magically know. That way, they'll be more likely to be there for you when you need them. ✿

Not even the best batters can hit them all.

> —**VIRNE BEATRICE "JACKIE" MITCHELL**, THE 17-YEAR-OLD GIRL WHO STRUCK OUT BABE RUTH AND LOU GEHRIG IN 1931

I don't believe in perfection. I don't think there is such a thing.

> —**REESE WITHERSPOON**, ACTOR

I think my head's on pretty straight, and I'm pretty realistic about things.

> —**SCARLETT JOHANSSON**, ACTOR

I had realized it was going to be very difficult to get a job in marine zoology, so I was beginning to think, "Okay. If you can't do that, then do something else."

> —**MEAVE LEAKEY**, PALEONTOLOGIST

I think knowing what you cannot do is more important than knowing what you can.

> —**LUCILLE BALL**, COMEDIAN AND ACTOR

You never conquer a mountain. You stand on the summit a few moments; then the wind blows your footprints away.

—**ARLENE BLUM**, MOUNTAINEER AND BIOPHYSICAL CHEMIST

Human beings aren't orchids; we must draw something from the soil we grow in.

—**SARA JEANNETTE DUNCAN**, AUTHOR AND JOURNALIST

Don't spend time beating on a wall, hoping to transform it into a door.

—**DR. LAURA SCHLESSINGER**, AUTHOR AND COMMENTATOR

Wisdom never kicks at the iron walls it can't bring down.

—**OLIVE SCHREINER**, SOUTH AFRICAN POLITICAL ACTIVIST AND NOVELIST

It is impossible to control creation.

> —**EVELYN SCOTT**, NOVELIST AND
> PLAYWRIGHT

Let us accept truth, even when it surprises us and alters our views.

> —**GEORGE SAND**, PEN NAME OF FRENCH
> NOVELIST AND FEMINIST AMANDINE DUPIN

A pint can't hold a quart—if it holds a pint it is doing all that can be expected of it.

> —**MARGARET DELAND**, NOVELIST AND POET

What had seemed easy in imagination was rather hard in reality.

> —**LUCY MAUD MONTGOMERY**, CANADIAN
> AUTHOR

Pioneers may be picturesque figures, but they are often rather lonely ones.

> —**NANCY ASTOR**, AMERICAN, FIRST WOMAN
> TO SERVE AS A MEMBER OF PARLIAMENT

Even I don't wake up looking like Cindy Crawford.
> —**CINDY CRAWFORD**, SUPERMODEL

Some people probably think actresses dress up everywhere they go. I'm in sweatpants half the time with my hair in a ponytail.
> —**SELENA GOMEZ**, ACTOR

We would worry less about what others think of us if we realized how seldom they do.
> —**ETHEL BARRETT**, CHRISTIAN STORYTELLER

Truth, however bitter, can be accepted, and woven into a design for living.
> —**AGATHA CHRISTIE**, ENGLISH MYSTERY WRITER

A fool or idiot is one who expects things to happen that never can happen.
> —**GEORGE ELIOT**, PEN NAME OF ENGLISH NOVELIST MARY ANN EVANS

Don't fool yourself that you are going to have it all. You are not. Psychologically, having it all is not even a valid concept. The marvelous thing about human beings is that we are perpetually reaching for the stars. The more we have, the more we want. And for this reason, we never have it all.

—DR. JOYCE BROTHERS, ADVICE COLUMNIST

Your goal should be out of reach but not out of sight.

—ANITA DEFRANTZ, OLYMPIC ROWER

Chapter 3

No Time for Negativity

Always thinking negative thoughts can really mess up your life.

If you tell yourself, "I'm know we're going to lose that soccer match tomorrow," you could end up so stressed out that you don't sleep well at night. You might then be so tired the next day that you don't play well.

If you tell yourself, "I know I'll never get a part in the school play," you might just talk yourself out of even trying out for a role. Or, you might try out but be so full of stage fright that you end up blowing your audition!

Your thoughts affect your feelings, your feelings affect your actions, and your actions affect a *lot* of what happens to you. So doesn't it make sense to start out with positive thoughts?

Whenever you find yourself thinking icky, depressing, negative thoughts, ask yourself these questions:

- Are my thoughts based on real facts, or just my imaginary fears?

- Is there anything I can do to fix things?

- If I can't do anything to fix things, will worrying change anything?

- How would I behave if I were thinking more positively?

Consider what these famous women learned about overcoming negativity. ✿

I used to wail and moan and cry, and little things were blown up into being big things. I don't know how my parents stood it, really. I've grown up a bit. I've had to.

—EMMA WATSON, ENGLISH ACTOR

I know I'm not going to make any money out of it. I know I'm not going to be famous.

—J. K. ROWLING (SPEAKING TO HER LITERARY AGENT AFTER SIGNING THE PUBLISHING CONTRACT FOR THE FIRST *HARRY POTTER* NOVEL)

Hate is like acid. It can damage the vessel in which it is stored as well as destroy the object on which it is poured.

—ANN LANDERS, ADVICE COLUMNIST

There are seeds of self-destruction in all of us that will bear only unhappiness if allowed to grow.

—DOROTHEA BRANDE, EDITOR

We have seen too much defeatism, too much pessimism, too much of a negative approach.

>—MARGO JONES, THEATER DIRECTOR

Keep your face to the sunshine and you cannot see the shadow.

>—HELEN KELLER, THE FIRST DEAFBLIND
> PERSON TO GRADUATE FROM COLLEGE

To think of losing is to lose already.

>—SYLVIA TOWNSEND WARNER, ENGLISH
> AUTHOR

The trouble with most people is that they think with their hopes or fears or wishes rather than with their minds.

>—NANCY ASTOR, AMERICAN, FIRST WOMAN
> TO SERVE AS A MEMBER OF PARLIAMENT

If you banish fear, nothing terribly bad can happen to you.

>—MARGARET BOURKE-WHITE,
> PHOTOJOURNALIST

Jealousy is no more than feeling alone against smiling enemies.

—**ELIZABETH BOWEN**, ENGLISH-IRISH
NOVELIST AND SHORT STORY WRITER

The key to change . . . is to let go of fear.

—**ROSANNE CASH**, SINGER AND SONGWRITER

Concern should drive us into action, not into depression.

—**KAREN HORNEY**, GERMAN PSYCHOLOGIST

Chapter 4

BEING THANKFUL

When was the last time you gave thanks for the good things in your life? (And don't say "On Thanksgiving"—everybody is thankful on *that* day!)

Some girls get so focused on the little annoying problems in their lives, they completely forget about everything that's going *right*. You can always find something to be grateful for, even when you're having one of those really, really bad days. Just thinking about those things can sometimes turn that bad day into a slightly better day.

Write down a few things every day that you're really thankful for. Think of the people you're happy to have as a part of your world, or make a list of the unique talents you have. Once you

put these things in writing, they'll be easier to remember the next time you're feeling down.

Now that you've written your gratitude, try speaking it out loud. Tell your friends or family members how much they mean to you. Hearing how much you appreciate them can be a great way to brighten their day. Tomorrow, they might return the favor! ☼

The day I got my first letter from a fan, I felt like I'd been touched by an angel.

—**SELENA GOMEZ**, ACTOR

I couldn't do it without my family.

—**VANESSA ANNE HUDGENS**, ACTOR

For the rest of my life I'm going to trust that God is always at work in all things, and give Him thanks long before my simplest prayers are answered.

—**NANCY PARKER BRUMMETT**, CHRISTIAN WRITER

Glee! The great storm is over!

—**EMILY DICKINSON**, POET

Joy is what happens to us when we allow ourselves to recognize how good things really are.

—**MARIANNE WILLIAMSON**, SPIRITUAL ACTIVIST, AUTHOR, AND LECTURER

Gratitude unlocks the fullness of life. It turns what we have into enough, and more. It turns denial into acceptance, chaos to order, confusion to clarity. It can turn a meal into a feast, a house into a home, a stranger into a friend. Gratitude makes sense of our past, brings peace for today, and creates a vision for tomorrow.

> —**MELODY BEATTIE**, SELF-HELP AUTHOR

Blessed are those who can give without remembering and take without forgetting.

> —**ELIZABETH ASQUITH BIBESCO**, ENGLISH WRITER

Remember that not to be happy is not to be grateful.

> —**ELIZABETH CARTER**, ENGLISH POET AND TRANSLATOR

We must give ourselves more earnestly and intelligently and generously than we have to the happy duty of appreciation.

> —**MARIANA GRISWOLD VAN RENSSELAER**, AUTHOR

It made me gladsome to be getting some education, it being like a big window opening.

— **MARY WEBB**, ENGLISH NOVELIST

Too much of a good thing can be wonderful.

— **MAE WEST**, ACTOR

Some memories are realities, and are better than anything that can ever happen to one again.

— **WILLA CATHER**, AUTHOR

As the dew to the blossom, the bud to the bee,

As the scent to the rose, are those memories to me.

— **AMELIA WELBY**, POET

Gratitude brings joy and laughter into your life and into the lives of all those around you.

— **EILEEN CADDY**, SCOTTISH WRITER

My gratitude for good writing is unbounded; I'm grateful for it the way I'm grateful for the ocean.

— **ANNE LAMOTT**, AUTHOR

Enjoy the successes that you have, and don't be too hard on yourself when you don't do well. Too many times we beat up on ourselves. Just relax and enjoy it.

—**PATTY SHEEHAN**, PROFESSIONAL GOLFER

No matter what accomplishments you make, somebody helps you.

—**ALTHEA GIBSON**, TENNIS PLAYER

Silent gratitude isn't much use to anyone.

—**GLADYS BRONWYN STERN**, ENGLISH NOVELIST

My father got me strong and straight and slim

And I give thanks to him.

My mother bore me glad and sound and sweet,

I kiss her feet.

—**MARGUERITE WILKINSON**, POET

Normal day, let me be aware of the treasure you are. Let me learn from you, love you, bless you before you depart. Let me not pass you by in quest of some rare and perfect tomorrow. Let me hold you while I may, for it may not always be so.

—**MARY JEAN IRION**, AUTHOR

I am in debt to my readers . . . What would have become of me if no one had wanted to read my books?

—**SELMA LAGERLÖF**, SWEDISH, FIRST WOMAN TO WIN THE NOBEL PRIZE IN LITERATURE

Chapter 5

People Need You

As a young person, you really have to depend on other people for a lot of stuff—food and shelter, transportation, education, love, and support. Sometimes, we get so caught up in what we need from others that we forget that those people need things from us, too.

No matter who you are, you probably have a younger family member or neighbor who secretly looks up to you. She might not show it—in fact, she might even act a little bratty sometimes, because she feels inferior around you!

Adults need you, too. Grandparents and other older adults need you to listen to their stories so that they can share their wisdom and experience. Teachers feel fulfilled when they know the work they do is making a difference in your life. And they might not always take the time to

say it, but parents are frequently thinking about how their kids are the best thing that ever happened to them.

You probably never realized how important you are to all these people, did you? Give yourself a pat on the back for being the type of girl others can't live without! ✿

I see their souls, and I hold them in my hands, and because I love them they weigh nothing.

—**PEARL BAILEY**, SINGER AND ACTOR

One's life has value so long as one attributes value to the life of others, by means of love, friendship, indignation, and compassion.

—**SIMONE DE BEAUVOIR**, FRENCH AUTHOR
AND PHILOSOPHER

I'd like people to think of me as someone who cares about them.

—**DIANA**, PRINCESS OF WALES

Listen long enough and the person will generally come up with an adequate solution.

—**MARY KAY ASH**, BUSINESSWOMAN AND
FOUNDER OF MARY KAY COSMETICS

We deceive ourselves when we believe that only weakness needs support. Strength needs it far more.

—**ANNE-SOPHIE SWETCHINE**, RUSSIAN
MYSTIC

It is only in the giving of oneself to others that we truly live.

—**ETHEL PERCY ANDRUS,** FIRST FEMALE HIGH SCHOOL PRINCIPAL IN THE STATE OF CALIFORNIA

There is nothing to make you like other human beings so much as doing things for them.

—**ZORA NEALE HURSTON,** AUTHOR AND FOLKLORIST

Fill the cup of happiness for others, and there will be enough overflowing to fill yours to the brim.

—**ROSE PASTOR STOKES,** FEMINIST

Nothing liberates our greatness like the desire to help, the desire to serve.

—**MARIANNE WILLIAMSON,** SPIRITUAL ACTIVIST, AUTHOR, AND LECTURER

We want to create hope for the person. . . . We must give hope, always hope.

> —**MOTHER TERESA**, ALBANIAN MISSIONARY
> AND HUMANITARIAN

Miss no single opportunity of making some small sacrifice, here by a smiling look, there by a kindly word; always doing the smallest right and doing it all for love.

> —**THÉRÈSE OF LISIEUX**, FRENCH MEMOIRIST
> AND SPIRITUAL ICON

After the verb "to Love," "to Help" is the most beautiful verb in the world.

> —**BERTHA VON SUTTNER**, AUSTRO-
> HUNGARIAN, FIRST WOMAN TO WIN THE
> NOBEL PEACE PRIZE

We ought to be doing all we can to make it possible for every child to fulfill his or her God-given potential.

> —**HILLARY RODHAM CLINTON**,
> SENATOR, FORMER FIRST LADY, AND U.S.
> PRESIDENTIAL CANDIDATE

If you feed a man a meal, you only feed him for a day—but if you teach a man to grow food, you feed him for a lifetime.

>—**MILDRED LISETTE NORMAN**, "PEACE PILGRIM," PEACE ACTIVIST

One of my main goals on the planet is to encourage people to empower themselves.

>—**OPRAH WINFREY**, TALK SHOW HOST AND MEDIA MOGUL

Female friendships that work are relationships in which we help each other belong to ourselves.

>—**LOUISE BERNIKOW**, JOURNALIST AND WOMEN'S HISTORY LECTURER

You leave home to seek your fortune and, when you get it, you go home and share it with your family.

>—**ANITA BAKER**, SINGER AND SONGWRITER

Don't give advice unless you're asked.

>—**AMY ALCOTT**, PROFESSIONAL GOLFER

Don't forget that compared to a grownup person every baby is a genius. Think of the capacity to learn! The freshness, the temperament, the will of a baby a few months old!

   —**MAY SARTON**, POET, NOVELIST, AND MEMOIRIST

I've always thought that people need to feel good about themselves and I see my role as offering support to them, to provide some light along the way.

   —**DIANA**, PRINCESS OF WALES

We have to improve life, not just for those who have the most skills and those who know how to manipulate the system. But also for and with those who often have so much to give but never get the opportunity.

   —**DOROTHY HEIGHT**, EDUCATOR AND RECIPIENT OF THE CONGRESSIONAL GOLD MEDAL

Giving opens the way for receiving.

   —**FLORENCE SCOVEL SHINN**, AUTHOR AND MYSTIC

Chapter 6

BEST FRIENDS FOREVER

Are you one of those outgoing girls who hangs out with a ton of people? Or are you the more private type, who shares her feelings and dreams with only a few close friends?

No matter how many friends you have, you have to admit that the really great ones sure make life a lot more fun. Here are some tips on how to be a great friend:

- Try to keep in touch with old friends who have moved to different schools or neighborhoods.

- If you try to maintain a friendship, but the other person doesn't seem interested, don't worry about it. Sometimes people change, and letting go might just make things easier for everyone involved. Who knows? You might even renew your friendship in the years ahead.

- Being part of a clique can make you feel like you fit in, but it can also really limit your social life. Talk to the girls you hang out with, and ask if it would be cool if you invited some other girls to join the group.

- If you see a new girl at school, why not volunteer to show her around? You don't have to try to be her best buddy. Just be nice to her and help her meet other people.

- Never let other people bad-mouth or bully your friends. Friends always stick up for one another. ✿

True friends are those who really know you but love you anyway.

> —**EDNA BUCHANAN,** PULITZER PRIZE–
> WINNING JOURNALIST AND MYSTERY
> NOVELIST

It's the friends you can call up at 4:00 a.m. that matter.

> —**MARLENE DIETRICH,** ACTOR, SINGER, AND
> ENTERTAINER

There's no friend like someone who has known you since you were five.

> —**ANNE STEVENSON,** POET

Lots of people want to ride with you in the limo, but what you want is someone who will take the bus with you when the limo breaks down.

> —**OPRAH WINFREY,** TALK SHOW HOST AND
> MEDIA MOGUL

The growth of true friendship may be a lifelong affair.

> —SARAH ORNE JEWETT, NOVELIST AND
> SHORT STORY WRITER

We need old friends to help us grow old and new friends to help us stay young.

> —LETTY COTTIN POGREBIN, WRITER AND
> JOURNALIST

Friends are the thermometer by which we may judge the temperature of our fortunes.

> —MARGARET POWER, IRISH NOVELIST

And we find at the end of a perfect day,

The soul of a friend we've made.

> —CARRIE JACOBS-BOND, SINGER AND
> SONGWRITER

That is the best—to laugh with someone because you think the same things are funny.

> —GLORIA VANDERBILT, ARTIST AND ACTOR

Love is like the wild-rose briar;

Friendship is like the holly-tree.

The holly is dark when the rose briar blooms,

But which will bloom most constantly?

> —**EMILY BRONTË,** ENGLISH NOVELIST AND
> POET

If you want an accounting of your worth, count your friends.

> —**MERRY BROWNE,** AUTHOR

If I don't have friends, then I ain't nothing.

> —**BILLIE HOLIDAY,** JAZZ VOCALIST AND
> SONGWRITER

Success . . . depends on your ability to make and keep friends.

> —**SOPHIE TUCKER,** SINGER AND COMEDIAN

Friendship is an art, and very few persons are born with a natural gift for it.

> —**KATHLEEN NORRIS,** ROMANCE NOVELIST

I can trust my friends. . . . These people force me to examine myself, encourage me to grow.

—**CHER**, SINGER AND ACTOR

No person is your friend who demands your silence, or denies your right to grow.

—**ALICE WALKER**, PULITZER PRIZE–WINNING AUTHOR

A friend can tell you things you don't want to tell yourself.

—**FRANCES WARD WELLER**, CHILDREN'S BOOK AUTHOR

If we would build on a sure foundation in friendship, we must love friends for their sake rather than for our own.

—**CHARLOTTE BRONTË**, ENGLISH NOVELIST

Treat your friends as you do your picture, and place them in their best light.

—JENNIE JEROME CHURCHILL, MOTHER
    OF BRITISH PRIME MINISTER WINSTON
    CHURCHILL

A friend in need is a friend indeed.

—SUSAN FERRIER, SCOTTISH NOVELIST

Plant a seed of friendship; reap a bouquet of happiness.

—LOIS L. KAUFMAN, AUTHOR

Chapter 7

DOING WHAT YOU DO BEST

What is the one thing you're really good at? Do you play a musical instrument? Are you a star athlete? A total brainiac? A gifted writer or artist?

Maybe you haven't quite found that one thing you're really good at. That's OK, too. It's *way* more important to try things and to work hard at them than it is to be number 1 at something. If you're having trouble finding yourself, try one or more of these tips:

- Get involved in different types of student organizations. Get on the staff of the school newspaper, run for student council, or maybe sign up for that ethnic club at your school.

- If you like being part of a group, try out for a team sport like soccer or basketball. If you're more of a loner, try one of the individual sports like cross-country or track and field.

- Although trying different things is important, don't just quit if things become boring or too challenging. "Sticking with it" through tough times is a great way to feel good about yourself and discover your true character. ✿

Are you a poet? Are you a writer? An accountant? Are you a musician? Are you a scientist? Are you a kid who cares? Whatever it is you are, you have some power to use that capability.

—**SYLVIA EARLE**, UNDERSEA EXPLORER

I really liked math and science in school and if I hadn't gotten that background, I wouldn't be where I am today.

—**CAROL BARTZ**, HEAD OF A SOFTWARE DEVELOPMENT COMPANY

I was excited about achieving a career in physics. My family thought the most desirable position for me would be as an elementary school teacher.

—**ROSALYN SUSSMAN YALOW**, PHYSICIST, WINNER OF THE NOBEL PRIZE IN MEDICINE

The great thing to learn about life is, first, not to do what you don't want to do, and, second, to do what you do want to do.

—**MARGARET ANDERSON**, LITERARY MAGAZINE EDITOR

There is a need to find and sing our own song, to stretch our limbs and shake them in a dance so wild that nothing can roost there, that stirs the yearning for solitary voyage.

—BARBARA LAZEAR ASCHER, ESSAYIST

I know a lot of people think it's monotonous, down the black lines over and over, but it's not if you're enjoying what you're doing. I love to swim and I love to train.

—TRACY CAULKINS, OLYMPIC GOLD MEDAL-
WINNING SWIMMER

Find something you're passionate about and keep tremendously interested in it.

—JULIA CHILD, COOK, AUTHOR, AND
TELEVISION PERSONALITY

We only do well the things we like doing.

—COLETTE, FRENCH NOVELIST

want to do it because I want to do it.

>—**AMELIA EARHART**, FIRST WOMAN TO FLY
> OVER THE ATLANTIC OCEAN

Duty is an icy shadow. It will freeze you. It cannot fill the heart's sanctuary.

>—**AUGUSTA EVANS**, NOVELIST

What I wanted was to be allowed to do the thing in the world that I did best—which I believed then and believe now is the greatest privilege there is. When I did that, success found me.

>—**DEBBI FIELDS**, FOUNDER OF MRS. FIELDS
> COOKIES

Follow what you love! Don't deign to ask what "they" are looking for out there. Ask what you have inside. Follow not your interests, which change, but what you are and what you love, which will and should not change.

>—**GEORGIE ANNE GEYER**, SYNDICATED
> NEWSPAPER COLUMNIST

The first duty of a human being is to assume the right relationship to society—more briefly, to find your real job, and do it.

—**CHARLOTTE PERKINS GILMAN**, AUTHOR, LECTURER, AND SOCIAL REFORMER

We don't know who we are until we see what we can do.

—**MARTHA GRIMES**, AUTHOR OF DETECTIVE NOVELS

The things that one most wants to do are the things that are probably most worth doing.

—**WINIFRED HOLTBY**, ENGLISH NOVELIST AND JOURNALIST

What really matters is what you do with what you have.

—**SHIRLEY LORD**, AUTHOR AND BEAUTY EDITOR

I am a writer because writing is the thing I do best.

—**FLANNERY O'CONNOR**, AUTHOR

I have the feeling when I write poetry that I am doing what I am supposed to do. You don't think about whether you're going to get money or fame, you just do it.

—**DORIS LUND**, AUTHOR

In the first grade, I already knew the pattern of my life. I didn't know the living of it, but I knew the line. . . . From the first day in school until the day I graduated, everyone gave me one hundred plus in art. Well, where do you go in life? You go to the place where you got one hundred plus.

—**LOUISE NEVELSON**, ARTIST AND SCULPTOR

I know that I haven't powers enough to divide myself into one who earns and one who creates.

—**TILLIE OLSEN**, WRITER AND FEMINIST

The best career advice given to the young . . . is "Find out what you like doing best and get someone to pay you for doing it."

—**KATHARINE WHITEHORN**, ENGLISH
    JOURNALIST

Chapter 8

YOU CAN DO IT

Has there ever been something you really wanted to do or have—but you never even tried for it, because you were afraid you might fail?

Sometimes the biggest obstacle that stands between you and the things you want is your own self-doubt. To overcome those doubts, follow in the footsteps of daring girls everywhere:

Dream big! Don't just try easy things because you'll know you'll succeed. Set the bar high for yourself. If you succeed, you'll feel great. And if you fall short of your goal, you'll still have done much more than you would have if you had taken the easy route.

Make a plan. Plans turn dreams into goals. Write down a list of all the steps you'd have to take to achieve your dream. Then, tackle those steps one at a time. Breaking big dreams down into little steps will make them seem more "doable."

Work every day at your plan. Don't expect overnight success. Just work hard on your plan, and you'll get a little closer to your dream each day!

Don't get discouraged! Sometimes a part of your plan won't work. Don't lose hope—sit down again and rewrite that step, or the next few steps, until you can get back on track. ✿

Each time I leaped I seemed to touch the sky and when I regained earth it seemed to be mine alone.

—**JOSEPHINE BAKER**, SINGER

There is a place in God's sun for the youth "farthest down" who has the vision, the determination, and the courage to reach it.

—**MARY MCLEOD BETHUNE**, EDUCATOR

Nearly every glamorous, wealthy, successful career woman you might envy now started out as some kind of schlepp.

—**HELEN GURLEY BROWN**, AUTHOR, PUBLISHER, AND BUSINESSWOMAN

The fact that I was a girl never damaged my ambitions to be a pope or an emperor.

—**WILLA CATHER**, AUTHOR

Tell them that as soon as I can walk I'm going to fly!

—**BESSIE COLEMAN**, FIRST FEMALE AFRICAN AMERICAN AIRPLANE PILOT

He who demands little gets it.

—**ELLEN GLASGOW**, PULITZER PRIZE–
WINNING NOVELIST

I probably hold the distinction of being one movie star who, by all laws of logic, should never have made it. At each stage of my career, I lacked the experience.

—**AUDREY HEPBURN**, ACTOR AND
HUMANITARIAN

If we want a free and peaceful world, if we want to make the deserts bloom and man grow to greater dignity as a human being—we can do it.

—**ELEANOR ROOSEVELT**, FORMER FIRST LADY
AND CIVIL RIGHTS ACTIVIST

You can change your beliefs so they empower your dreams and desires. Create a strong belief in yourself and what you want.

—**MARCIA WIEDER**, DREAM COACH

I used to tremble from nerves so badly that the only way I could hold my head steady was to lower my chin practically to my chest and look up at Bogie. That was the beginning of "The Look."

 —LAUREN BACALL, ACTOR

Whenever there is chaos, it creates wonderful thinking. I consider chaos a gift.

 —SEPTIMA POINSETTE CLARK, EDUCATOR
  AND CIVIL RIGHTS ACTIVIST

Everyone has inside of him a piece of good news. The good news is that you don't know how great you can be! How much you can love! What you can accomplish! And what your potential is!

 —ANNE FRANK, GERMAN-BORN DIARIST AND
  HOLOCAUST VICTIM

A willing heart adds feather to the heel.

 —JOANNA BAILLIE, SCOTTISH POET AND
  PLAYWRIGHT

Let the world know you as you are, not as you think you should be, because sooner or later, if you are posing, you will forget the pose, and then where are you?

—**FANNY BRICE**, COMEDIAN, SINGER, AND ACTOR

I am a woman who understands the necessity of an impulse whose goal or origin still lie beyond me.

—**OLGA BROUMAS**, GREEK POET

If you're a champion, you have to have it in your heart.

—**CHRIS EVERT**, PROFESSIONAL TENNIS PLAYER

We have to dare to be ourselves, however frightening or strange that self may prove to be.

—**MAY SARTON**, POET, NOVELIST, AND MEMOIRIST

Nobody can be exactly like me. Sometimes even I
have trouble doing it.

—**TALLULAH BANKHEAD**, ACTOR

If you are going to think black, think positive about
it. Don't think down on it, or think it is something in
your way. And this way, when you really do want to
stretch out and express how beautiful black is, everybody will hear you.

—**LEONTYNE PRICE**, OPERA SINGER

Oh, I'm so inadequate. And I love myself!

—**MEG RYAN**, ACTOR

No matter how lonely you get or how many birth
announcements you receive, the trick is not to get
frightened. There's nothing wrong with being alone.

—**WENDY WASSERSTEIN**, PLAYWRIGHT

Chapter 9

DARE TO BE FIRST

Being the first girl to do something can be pretty scary. Going first not only means that lots of other people may be watching you, it also means that those people may be waiting to see how you do before *they* try it. So, not only will you be afraid of making a fool of yourself, you might be worried about letting all those other people down!

But going first can also be exciting. People will think you are really confident and brave (even if you're secretly scared out of your mind). We all tend to remember the first person to do something, so going first can be your ticket to popularity. And since some opportunities are available only to the girl who steps up first, being brave can introduce you to fun things that everyone else ends up missing out on.

Make a list of things that you could try for the first time, before anyone else does. Maybe it's something simple like being the first person in school to sign a petition. Or, maybe you can be the first girl in your family to decide to go to college. Whether it's something small or big, find something no one else has done yet, and step to the front of the line! ⚙

This is a way to push myself to another level.

> —**ANNIKA SÖRENSTAM**, FIRST FEMALE
> GOLFER TO COMPETE IN A MEN'S PGA
> EVENT IN 58 YEARS

When you win, people find fault. They say, "Oh, she just wins because she's a wave hog," or "She's too aggressive." I used to think, how can I win if I'm not aggressive?

> —**MARGO (GODFREY) OBERG**, FIRST FEMALE
> BIG-WAVE SURFER

I wouldn't be here if I didn't think I could make it all the way. I've known since I was 10 I wanted to play in the major leagues.

> —**ILA BORDERS**, FIRST WOMAN TO PITCH IN
> A MEN'S PRO LEAGUE DURING THE REGULAR
> SEASON

All the good things in my life have happened because of racing. It helped me develop an identity.

> —**LYN ST. JAMES**, FIRST FEMALE TO COMPETE
> FULL-TIME ON THE INDY PRO RACING
> CIRCUIT

While lying on the ledge half-asleep, I thought about the various people who inspired me throughout my life. These thoughts helped me cultivate the faith and energy I needed to persevere.

> —**LYNN HILL**, FIRST AND ONLY PERSON TO FREE-CLIMB THE "NOSE" ROUTE OF YOSEMITE'S EL CAPITAN IN UNDER 24 HOURS

I had faith in myself. I had always felt that I could become prime minister if I wanted.

> —**BENAZIR BHUTTO**, FIRST ELECTED WOMAN TO LEAD A MUSLIM STATE (PAKISTAN)

Who would have thought 20, 10, five years ago, that Chile would elect a woman president? Thank you for inviting me to lead this voyage.

> —**MICHELLE BACHELET**, FIRST FEMALE PRESIDENT OF CHILE

Believe that you can, but plan. It will not fall in your lap.

> —**ANTONIA NOVELLO**, FIRST FEMALE SURGEON GENERAL OF THE UNITED STATES

There's nothing better than being yourself.

> —**CRISTINA FERNÁNDEZ DE KIRCHNER,**
> FIRST ELECTED FEMALE PRESIDENT OF
> ARGENTINA

I was the first woman to be elected to a Presidency in the world and I think that it is outstanding that Icelanders had the guts to do this and lead the way.

> —**VIGDÍS FINNBOGADÓTTIR,** FIRST FEMALE
> PRESIDENT OF ICELAND

I am Violeta Barrios de Chamorro, and I don't have to ask anyone's opinion of anything. Period.

> —**VIOLETA BARRIOS DE CHAMORRO,** FIRST
> FEMALE PRESIDENT OF NICARAGUA

[My election was] a breakthrough . . . not just for me but for women. It was a great boost for the confidence of women.

> —**MARY ROBINSON,** FIRST FEMALE PRESIDENT
> OF THE REPUBLIC OF IRELAND

Do the best you can in every task, no matter how unimportant it may seem at the time.

—**SANDRA DAY O'CONNOR**, FIRST FEMALE JUSTICE OF THE U.S. SUPREME COURT

If you have the chance to explore and see what things there are to do out there . . . then follow where you feel the most passion, the future tends to take care of itself.

—**LIBBY RIDDLES**, FIRST FEMALE MUSHER TO WIN THE IDITAROD TRAIL SLED DOG RACE

If you love it then while you are doing it you are a true expression of yourself and your time and your story. You are authentic.

—**LINA WERTMÜLLER**, ITALIAN FILMMAKER AND FIRST WOMAN NOMINATED FOR AN ACADEMY AWARD FOR BEST DIRECTOR

I always wanted to be a mathematician.

—**DUSA MCDUFF**, ENGLISH, FIRST WINNER OF THE RUTH LYTTLE SATTER PRIZE FOR HER CONTRIBUTION TO THE FIELD OF MATHEMATICS

Nobody took me seriously. They wondered why in the world I wanted to be a chemist when no women were doing that.

—**GERTRUDE BELLE ELION**, NOBEL PRIZE WINNER AND FIRST WOMAN TO BE INDUCTED INTO THE NATIONAL INVENTORS HALL OF FAME

Chapter 10

WHOSE LIFE *IS* IT, ANYWAY?

Have you ever noticed how other people are always ready to give you advice—even when you haven't asked them for any?

Never forget that you are responsible for your own decisions. Looking to other people for advice might give you important insights, but you should never leave your dreams and goals in the hands of others. It's your life, after all!

Here's a neat trick to use when you can't decide whether to follow the crowd or to follow your heart:

> *Think about your problem, and then write down what your instincts tell you to do about it. After you write down your heart's solution, create two columns—one with a list of the worst things that could happen*

if you follow your own advice, and then another list right next to it of the best things that could happen.

Seeing things listed side by side can have a big effect on how you see your problem. What you'll probably realize is that the very worst thing that could happen really isn't that big of a deal after all. Or, maybe you'll realize that you have way more to lose than to gain by taking a foolish risk. Either way, putting things down on paper is a great way to compare your options. ✿

I don't feed into anyone's idea of who I should be.

—JESSICA ALBA, ACTOR

Being cool is being your own self, not doing something that someone else is telling you to do.

—VANESSA ANNE HUDGENS, ACTOR

I don't want to be a passenger in my own life.

—DIANE ACKERMAN, WRITER AND NATURALIST

Independence is happiness.

—SUSAN B. ANTHONY, SUFFRAGIST

When I saw something that needed doing, I did it.

—NELLIE CASHMAN, GOLD PROSPECTOR

No one is in control of your happiness but you; therefore, you have the power to change anything about yourself or your life that you want to change.

—BARBARA DE ANGELIS, AUTHOR AND RELATIONSHIP EXPERT

I never really address myself to any image anybody has of me. That's like fighting with ghosts.
—SALLY FIELD, ACTOR

I don't follow precedent, I establish it.
—FANNY ELLEN HOLTZMANN, LAWYER

The thing women have got to learn is that nobody gives you power. You just take it.
—ROSEANNE BARR, ACTOR AND COMEDIAN

Who ever walked behind anyone to freedom?
—HAZEL SCOTT, PIANIST AND SINGER

I am learning that if I just go on accepting the framework for life that others have given me, if I fail to make my own choices, the reason for my life will be missing. I will be unable to recognize that which I have the power to change.
—LIV ULLMANN, NORWEGIAN ACTOR

You are in the driver's seat of your life and can point your life down any road you want to travel. You can go as fast or as slow as you want to go—and you can change the road you're on at any time.

—JINGER HEATH, ENTREPRENEUR AND
    AUTHOR

I resolved to take Fate by the throat and shake a living out of her.

—LOUISA MAY ALCOTT, AUTHOR

He alone is great

Who by a life heroic conquers fate.

—SARAH KNOWLES BOLTON, WRITER

When I get logical, and I don't trust my instincts, that's when I get into trouble.

—ANGELINA JOLIE, ACTOR

I think that somehow, we learn who we really are and then live with that decision.

—ELEANOR ROOSEVELT, FORMER FIRST LADY
    AND CIVIL RIGHTS ACTIVIST

A lot of girls feel like they need to wear what every-one else is wearing. But it's good to have your own trend. People will start following it!

—**MILEY CYRUS**, ACTOR, SINGER, AND SONGWRITER

There are definitely people I respect and I love their music, but there was never really an artist that I said, "I want to be just like them, I love the way their career is going. I love their music." It wasn't really like that. I wanted to be like myself.

—**HILARY DUFF**, ACTOR, SINGER, AND SONGWRITER

Everyone is trying to put me out to pasture. Maybe I just haven't found the right field yet!

—**JEANNIE LONGO-CIPRELLI**, FRENCH, 12-TIME WORLD CHAMPION CYCLIST

My mother told me to be a lady. And for her, that meant be your own person, be independent.

—**RUTH BADER GINSBERG**, U.S. SUPREME COURT JUSTICE

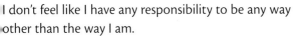
I don't feel like I have any responsibility to be any way other than the way I am.

—SCARLET JOHANSSON, ACTOR

Ninety per cent of how you learn is watching great people. When you are surrounded by good actors it lifts your performance.

—NATALIE PORTMAN, ACTOR

The two important things I did learn were that you are as powerful and strong as you allow yourself to be, and that the most difficult part of any endeavour is taking the first step, making the first decision.

—ROBYN DAVIDSON, AUSTRALIAN EXPLORER
    AND TRAVEL WRITER

Chapter 11

WHAT REALLY MATTERS?

Ask most girls what they worry about, and they'll probably tell you:

a) grades
b) the future
c) what other kids think about them

But is taking an easy class (and getting an A) better than challenging yourself (and getting a B) in a more difficult class?

Does worrying about the future really solve anything?

Can you really control what other people think about you?

Sometimes our silly worries distract us from the things that matter most: family, friends, good health, faith, and the fact that every day is a

blessing. Every minute we spend stressing out about things we can't control is a minute that could've been spent on those more important things.

Take a minute today to stop and smell the roses. Really savor your meals today, rather than eating on the run. Say "hi" to a neighbor, just to be nice. Give a family member a big hug. Smile at everyone you pass in the hallways at school. It's the little pleasures of each day—not those big scary things in the future—that make life so wonderful. ⚙

Moderation. Small helpings. Sample a little bit of everything. These are the secrets of happiness and good health.

—JULIA CHILD, COOK, AUTHOR, AND
   TELEVISION PERSONALITY

I am beginning to learn that it is the sweet, simple things of life which are the real ones after all.

—LAURA INGALLS WILDER, AUTHOR

The best things in life aren't things.

—ANN LANDERS, ADVICE COLUMNIST

It is good to have an end to journey toward, but it is the journey that matters in the end.

—URSULA K. LE GUIN, AUTHOR

I don't want to make money. I just want to be wonderful.

—MARILYN MONROE, ACTOR

Getting what you go after is success; but liking it while you are getting it is happiness.

—BERTHA DAMON, AUTHOR

Someone once asked me what I regarded as the three most important requirements for happiness. My answer was: "A feeling that you have been honest with yourself and those around you; a feeling that you have done the best you could both in your personal life and in your work; and the ability to love others."

—ELEANOR ROOSEVELT, FORMER FIRST LADY
AND CIVIL RIGHTS ACTIVIST

There is a gigantic difference between earning a great deal of money and being rich.

—MARLENE DIETRICH, ACTOR, SINGER, AND
ENTERTAINER

What matters most is that we learn from living.

—DORIS LESSING, ENGLISH AUTHOR

There are only two things that are absolute realities,
love and knowledge, and you can't escape them.

> —**OLIVE SCHREINER**, SOUTH AFRICAN
> POLITICAL ACTIVIST AND NOVELIST

There is only one happiness in life, to love and be
loved.

> —**GEORGE SAND**, PEN NAME OF FRENCH
> NOVELIST AND FEMINIST AMANDINE DUPIN

A sure way to lose happiness, I found, is to want it at
the expense of everything else.

> —**BETTE DAVIS**, ACTOR

Wealth consists not in having great possessions but
in having few wants.

> —**ESTHER DE WAAL**, CHRISTIAN SCHOLAR

I'm not someone who sacrifices all for the cinema; my
life will always be more important.

> —**NATALIE PORTMAN**, ACTOR

I need nothing but God, and to lose myself in the heart of God.

    —ST. MARGARET MARY ALACOQUE, FRENCH MYSTIC

There is nothing like staying at home for real comfort.

    —JANE AUSTEN, ENGLISH NOVELIST

What would life be without art?

    —SARAH BERNHARDT, FRENCH STAGE ACTOR

Small kindnesses, small courtesies, small considerations . . . give a greater charm to the character than the display of great talents and accomplishments.

    —MARY ANN KELTY, ENGLISH AUTHOR

Eating is not merely a material pleasure. Eating well gives a spectacular joy to life.

    —ELSA SCHIAPARELLI, ITALIAN-BORN CLOTHING DESIGNER

Age is something that doesn't matter, unless you are a cheese.

—**BILLIE BURKE**, ACTOR

I don't think about whether people will remember me or not. I've been an okay person. I've learned a lot. I've taught people a thing or two. That's what's important.

—**JULIA CHILD**, COOK, AUTHOR, AND
TELEVISION PERSONALITY

Chapter 12

It's Up to You

It's great to dream of a better life, but you can't wait around for some fairy godmother to come along to make it happen! It's up to *you* to bring about the changes that you want to see.

Have you ever wished you had more spending money? Getting a part-time job is more effective than begging your parents for a bigger allowance. Even if you're not quite old enough for a "real" job, there are all sorts of things you can do to earn a little extra money . . . from delivering newspapers to babysitting to helping an elderly neighbor with his or her chores.

If your social or dating life kind of stinks right now, think about someone you know who you think would be fun to hang out with, and give that person a call. If that seems a little too scary, you can always text or e-mail them, or leave a

note for them on MySpace, Facebook, or what-ever social networking site they use.

And if you feel like your voice isn't being heard at school or where you worship, there are prob-ably other girls just like you thinking the same thing. Advisers, teachers, and clergy might be able to help you to start a new club or youth group.

Whatever it is, if you see something that needs doing, then you're probably just the girl to do it! ⚙

If you have your eye set on somebody, don't beat around the bush.

—**VANESSA ANNE HUDGENS**, ACTOR

Every action we take, everything we do, is either a victory or defeat in the struggle to become what we want to be.

—**ANNE BYRHHE**, EDUCATOR

Happiness is not something you get, but something you do.

—**MARCELENE COX**, AUTHOR

Getting fit is a political act—you are taking charge of your life.

—**JANE FONDA**, ACTOR AND ACTIVIST

It is easier to live life through someone else than to become complete yourself.

—**BETTY FRIEDAN**, FEMINIST, ACTIVIST, AND WRITER

As far as beauty is concerned, in order to be confident we must accept that the way we look and feel is our own responsibility.

—**SOPHIA LOREN**, ITALIAN ACTOR

Exude happiness and you will feel it back a thousand times.

—**JOAN LUNDEN**, BROADCASTER

You are the product of your own brainstorm.

—**ROSEMARY KONNER STEINBAUM**, EDUCATOR

I am one of those people who are blessed with a nature which has to interfere. If I see a thing that needs doing I do it.

—**MARGERY ALLINGHAM**, ENGLISH NOVELIST

The willingness to accept responsibility for one's own life is the source from which self-respect springs.

—**JOAN DIDION**, ESSAYIST AND NOVELIST

If you don't like the way the world is, you change it. You have an obligation to change it. You just do it one step at a time.

—**MARIAN WRIGHT EDELMAN**, CIVIL RIGHTS AND CHILDREN'S RIGHTS ACTIVIST

You can only avoid responsibility for so long.

—**ROSARIO DAWSON**, ACTOR

Revolution begins with the self, in the self.

—**TONI CADE BAMBARA**, AUTHOR, SOCIAL ACTIVIST, AND PROFESSOR

We are accountable only to ourselves for what happens to us in our lives.

—**MILDRED NEWMAN**, AUTHOR

I attribute my success to this: I never gave or took an excuse.

—**FLORENCE NIGHTINGALE**, ENGLISH PIONEER OF MODERN NURSING

I made the decision. I'm accountable.

—JANET RENO, FIRST FEMALE ATTORNEY
GENERAL OF THE UNITED STATES

There are people who put their dreams in a little box and say, "Yes, I've got dreams, of course, I've got dreams." Then they put the box away and bring it out once in a while to look in it, and yep, they're still there. These are great dreams, but they never even get out of the box. It takes an uncommon amount of guts to put your dreams on the line, to hold them up and say, "How good or how bad am I?" That's where courage comes in.

—ERMA BOMBECK, HUMORIST

It's no good saying one thing and doing another.

—CATHERINE COOKSON, ENGLISH AUTHOR

Make the world better.

—LUCY STONE, ABOLITIONIST AND
SUFFRAGIST

Remember, no effort that we make to attain something beautiful is ever lost.

  —**HELEN KELLER,** THE FIRST DEAFBLIND
   PERSON TO GRADUATE FROM COLLEGE

Chapter 13

DOING THE RIGHT THING

Imagine this: you're taking a written quiz at school, and you see one of the smartest boys in class peeking at the paper of the girl who sits next to you. What do you do?

a) Tell your teacher.
b) Don't tell the teacher, but tell the boy later you saw him, and that he's a big creep.
c) Pretend you didn't see him, and never say a word to anyone. Why cause trouble?
d) Check out the girl's paper, too. If the smartest kid in class cheats, why can't you?

Doing the right thing can be tough sometimes. Cheating isn't fair, but no one likes to look like a big tattletale. Confronting the boy in person

may draw less attention, but it might not make him stop cheating, either. Pretending you didn't see him might be the easiest choice, but can you imagine what would happen to the world if everyone just ignored other people's bad behavior? And although you may hate cheaters, sometimes it seems like they're the ones who get ahead, while nice girls finish last.

Having a set of principles to guide you in life— and sticking to them—is an important part of building your character. When you're not sure about the right thing to do, just read these words from wise women who've been in exactly the same situation. ✿

The lesser evil is also evil.

> —**NAOMI MITCHISON,** SCOTTISH NOVELIST

I don't eat junk food and I don't think junk thoughts.

> —**MILDRED LISETTE NORMAN,** "PEACE
> PILGRIM," PEACE ACTIVIST

Truth is always exciting. Speak it, then; life is dull without it.

> —**PEARL S. BUCK,** AUTHOR

The naked truth is always better than the best-dressed lie.

> —**ANN LANDERS,** ADVICE COLUMNIST

The most exhausting thing in life is being insincere.

> —**ANNE MORROW LINDBERGH,** AVIATOR
> AND WRITER

Decide on what you think is right, and stick to it.

> —**GEORGE ELIOT,** PEN NAME OF ENGLISH
> NOVELIST MARY ANN EVANS

Conscience, as I understand it, is the impulse to do the right thing because it is right, regardless of personal ends, and has nothing whatever to do with the ability to distinguish between right and wrong.

—MARGARET COLLIER GRAHAM, AUTHOR

I cannot and will not cut my conscience to fit this year's fashions.

—LILLIAN HELLMAN, PLAYWRIGHT

It is well worth the efforts of a lifetime to have attained knowledge which justifies an attack on the root of all evil . . . which asserts that because forms of evil have always existed in society, therefore they must always exist.

—ELIZABETH BLACKWELL, ABOLITIONIST, WOMEN'S RIGHTS ACTIVIST, AND FIRST FEMALE DOCTOR IN THE UNITED STATES

Sow good services; sweet remembrances will grow from them.

—MADAME DE STAËL, SWISS AUTHOR

Power is the ability to do good things for others.

    —**BROOKE ASTOR**, PHILANTHROPIST

Character builds slowly, but it can be torn down with incredible swiftness.

    —**FAITH BALDWIN**, ROMANCE NOVELIST

Better to be without logic than without feeling.

    —**CHARLOTTE BRONTË**, ENGLISH NOVELIST

You cannot make yourself feel something you cannot feel, but you can make yourself do right in spite of your feelings.

    —**PEARL S. BUCK**, AUTHOR

Be pretty if you can, be witty if you must, but be gracious if it kills you.

    —**ELSIE DE WOLFE**, PIONEERING INTERIOR
      DECORATOR

Cruelty is the only sin.

—ELLEN GLASGOW, PULITZER PRIZING–
WINNING NOVELIST

Before a secret is told, one can often feel the weight
of it in the atmosphere.

—SUSAN GRIFFIN, WRITER AND EDUCATOR

I never fight, except against difficulties.

—HELEN KELLER, THE FIRST DEAFBLIND
PERSON TO GRADUATE FROM COLLEGE

Not observation of a duty but liberty itself is the
pledge that assures fidelity.

—ELLEN KEY, SWEDISH FEMINIST

A cruel story runs on wheels, and every hand oils the
wheels as they run.

—OUIDA, PEN NAME OF ENGLISH NOVELIST
MARIA LOUISE RAMÉE

Justice and judgment lie often a world apart.

> —**EMMELINE PANKHURST**, ENGLISH
> SUFFRAGIST

If you give your life as a wholehearted response to love, then love will wholeheartedly respond to you.

> —**MARIANNE WILLIAMSON**, SPIRITUAL
> ACTIVIST, AUTHOR, AND LECTURER

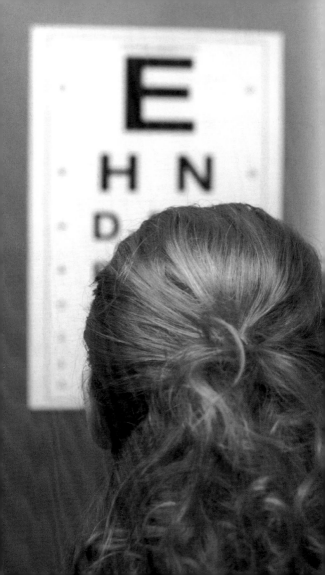

Chapter 14

CHANGING HOW YOU LOOK AT LIFE

Do you ever feel trapped in your own life? Like no matter how hard you try to give up a bad habit or turn over a new leaf, you always end up back in the same old place?

Sometimes it's not what you *do* in life that needs to change, it's how you *think* about your life. A good way to start is by really thinking about what the word "success" means to you.

If you only feel successful if you get an A in a class or get accepted into a big clique of girls, you may be setting yourself up for a disappointment. When did getting a B as a letter grade—or having just a few really close friends—make anyone a total loser?

It's much healthier to define success as living your best life every day—by studying hard (or maybe seeing a tutor if you think you need one), being kind to other people, avoiding negative people who always put you down, and so on. When you know you've done your best, you'll feel as though you accomplished your goals regardless of your grade point average or the size of your circle of friends. ✿

It is only in sorrow bad weather masters us; in joy we face the storm and defy it.

—**AMELIA BARR**, ENGLISH-AMERICAN
NOVELIST

I have found adventure in flying, in world travel, in business, and even close at hand. . . . Adventure is a state of mind—and spirit. It comes with faith, for with complete faith there is no fear of what faces you in life or death.

—**JACQUELINE COCHRAN**, PIONEERING
AVIATOR

There never was night that had no morn.

—**DINAH MARIA MULOCK CRAIK**, ENGLISH
NOVELIST AND POET

Hope is the thing with feathers

That perches in the soul,

And sings the tune without the words,

And never stops at all.

—**EMILY DICKINSON**, POET

My faith is important. I have nothing without it.

—**KATHY IRELAND**, ACTOR, MODEL, AND BUSINESSWOMAN

Someday the sun is going to shine down on me in some faraway place.

—**MAHALIA JACKSON**, GOSPEL SINGER

The real winners in life are the people who look at every situation with an expectation that they can make it work or make it better.

—**BARBARA PLETCHER**, BUSINESS AUTHOR

I have become my own version of an optimist. If I can't make it through one door, I'll go through another door—or I'll make a door. Something terrific will come no matter how dark the present.

—**JOAN RIVERS**, COMEDIAN AND TALK SHOW HOST

To some people, the impossible is impossible.

—**ELIZABETH ASQUITH BIBESCO**, ENGLISH WRITER

When I look to the future, it's so bright, it burns my eyes.

—**OPRAH WINFREY**, TALK SHOW HOST AND MEDIA MOGUL

Instead of looking at life as a narrowing funnel, we can see it ever widening to choose the things we want to do, to take the wisdom we've learned and create something.

—**LIZ CARPENTER**, WRITER, FEMINIST, AND PUBLIC SPEAKER

Others may argue about whether the world ends with a bang or a whimper. I just want to make sure mine doesn't end with a whine.

—**BARBARA GORDON**, AUTHOR AND SPEAKER

I discovered I always have choices and sometimes it's only a choice of attitude.

—**JUDITH M. KNOWLTON**, AUTHOR OF SELF-HELP BOOKS

If you believe, then you hang on.

> —**RUTH GORDON**, ACTOR AND WRITER

It's not the load that breaks you down, it's the way you carry it.

> —**LENA HORNE**, SINGER AND ACTOR

I'm not overweight, I'm just nine inches too short.

> —**SHELLEY WINTERS**, ACTOR

Nothing in life is so hard that you can't make it easier by the way you take it.

> —**ELLEN GLASGOW**, PULITZER PRIZE–
> WINNING NOVELIST

Never regret. If it's good, it's wonderful. If it's bad, it's experience.

> —**VICTORIA HOLT**, PEN NAME OF ENGLISH
> NOVELIST ELEANOR ALICE BURFORD

What you can't get out of, get into wholeheartedly.

> —**MIGNON MCLAUGHLIN**, JOURNALIST AND
> AUTHOR

We cannot alter facts, but we can alter our ways of looking at them.

—PHYLLIS BOTTOME, NOVELIST AND SHORT STORY WRITER

Without faith, nothing is possible. With it, nothing is impossible.

—MARY MCLEOD BETHUNE, EDUCATOR

All things are possible until they are proved impossible—and even the impossible may only be so, as of now.

—PEARL S. BUCK, AUTHOR

At first people refuse to believe that a strange new thing can be done, then they begin to hope it can be done, then they see it can be done—then it is done and all the world wonders why it was not done centuries ago.

—FRANCES HODGSON BURNETT, ENGLISH-AMERICAN PLAYWRIGHT AND AUTHOR

Chapter 15

TAKING RISKS

Some girls spend more time coming with up reasons *not* to do something than they do dreaming of things they'd *love* to do. These girls often find themselves stuck in a rut—having no real hobbies or interests, and leading a dull and boring social life.

There are a lot of reasons some girls act that way, but the biggest one is a fear of failure. If you come up with an excuse for not joining the concert choir, you never have to worry about someone hearing you sing off-key. If you never go up and talk to that one fun group of girls at school, you never have to worry about them thinking you're a big geek who could never fit into their "clique."

But taking risks—even when things don't turn out the way you hoped—can really change your

life. Being told you sing off-key may help you
realize that the clarinet (and not your voice)
is the musical instrument you need to perfect.
Getting rejected by the popular clique in school
may get you noticed by some other girls who
had the same experience—and *those* girls may
end up being your new best friends!

Whether you succeed or fail, the risks you take
will always present opportunities to learn and
grow. ✿

You don't become an Olympic champion without taking risks.

—**DOROTHY HAMILL**, OLYMPIC FIGURE
SKATER

If I make a fool of myself, who cares? I'm not frightened by anyone's perception of me.

—**ANGELINA JOLIE**, ACTOR

Security is not the meaning of my life. Great opportunities are worth the risks.

—**SHIRLEY HUFSTEDLER**, FORMER U.S.
SECRETARY OF EDUCATION

I am willing to put myself through anything; temporary pain or discomfort means nothing to me as long as I can see that the experience will take me to a new level. I am interested in the unknown, and the only path to the unknown is through breaking barriers, an often painful process.

—**DIANA NYAD**, LONG-DISTANCE SWIMMER

Providence has hidden a charm in difficult undertakings, which is appreciated only by those who dare to grapple with them.

—**ANNE-SOPHIE SWETCHINE**, RUSSIAN MYSTIC

Life is a risk.

—**DIANE VON FÜRSTENBERG**, FASHION DESIGNER

If you don't accept failure as a possibility, you don't set high goals, you don't branch out, you don't try— you don't take the risk.

—**ROSALYNN CARTER**, FORMER FIRST LADY

When in doubt, make a fool of yourself. There is a microscopically thin line between being brilliantly creative and acting like the most gigantic idiot on earth.

—**CYNTHIA HEIMEL**, PLAYWRIGHT AND AUTHOR

Take chances, make mistakes. That's how you grow. Pain nourishes your courage. You have to fail in order to practice being brave.

—MARY TYLER MOORE, ACTOR

And the trouble is, if you don't risk anything, you risk even more.

—ERICA JONG, AUTHOR AND EDUCATOR

We have to keep trying things we're not sure we can pull off. If we just do the things we know we can do . . . you don't grow as much. You gotta take those chances on making those big mistakes.

—CYBILL SHEPHERD, ACTOR

Act boldly and unseen forces will come to your aid.

—DOROTHEA BRANDE, EDITOR

Leap, and the net will appear.

—JULIA CAMERON, AUTHOR AND CREATIVITY EXPERT

Cowards falter, but danger is often overcome by those who nobly dare.

—QUEEN ELIZABETH I

Risk always brings its own rewards: the exhilaration of breaking through, of getting to the other side; the relief of a conflict healed; the clarity when a paradox dissolves.

—MARILYN FERGUSON, AUTHOR, MYSTIC, AND SPEAKER

Sometimes I think we can tell how important it is to risk by how dangerous it is to do so.

—SONIA JOHNSON, FEMINIST AND WRITER

Our whole way of life today is dedicated to the removal of risk. Cradle to grave we are supported, insulated, and isolated from the risks of life—and if we fall, our government stands ready with Band-Aids of every size.

—SHIRLEY TEMPLE BLACK, ACTOR, DIPLOMAT, AND AMBASSADOR

Dancing on the edge is the only place to be.

—**TRISHA BROWN**, CHOREOGRAPHER AND
DANCER

Traveling is like flirting with life. It's like saying, "I
would stay and love you, but I have to go; this is my
station."

—**LISA ST AUBIN DE TERÁN**, ENGLISH
NOVELIST AND MEMOIRIST

What one has not experienced, one will never understand in print.

—**ISADORA DUNCAN**, DANCER

I'm in love with the potential of miracles. For me, the
safest place is out on a limb.

—**SHIRLEY MACLAINE**, ACTOR AND MYSTIC

I never liked the middle ground—the most boring
place in the world.

—**LOUISE NEVELSON**, ARTIST AND SCULPTOR

Chapter 16

Keeping Your Dreams in Sight

It's funny how right at the moment when you feel like your life is going along pretty well, something screwy happens to mess everything up.

- You make the soccer team, but all the other girls on the team are such good players, you never get any time on the field.

- You get asked to the funnest dance of the year, but your parents tell you that you can't go because they need you stay home that night to babysit.

- You ace all the quizzes in math, but your teacher gives you a really hard final exam, and you end up with a B in the class.

There's no way you can control the world, especially the other people in it. Unplanned things are always going to happen. Rather than get discouraged and give up when things go wrong, just think of these events as detours on your journey. It might take you a little longer to reach your goals, and the goals might have changed a little by the time you get there. But if you keep your eyes open for all the "road signs" along the way, you'll reach your destination when many other girls end up lost. ✿

To have a reason to get up in the morning, it is necessary to possess a guiding principle.

—**JUDITH GUEST**, NOVELIST AND
SCREENWRITER

We can do whatever we wish to do provided our wish is strong enough. . . . What do you want most to do? That's what I have to keep asking myself, in the face of difficulties.

—**KATHERINE MANSFIELD**, NEW ZEALAND
–BORN SHORT STORY WRITER

You decide what it is you want to accomplish and then you lay out your plans to get there, and then you just do it. It's pretty straightforward.

—**NANCY DITZ**, OLYMPIC MARATHONER

Know what you want to do—then do it. Make straight for your goal and go undefeated in spirit to the end.

—**ERNESTINE SCHUMANN-HEINK**, OPERA
SINGER

A good goal is like a strenuous exercise—it makes you stretch.

—**MARY KAY ASH**, BUSINESSWOMAN AND
FOUNDER OF MARY KAY COSMETICS

The self-confidence one builds from achieving difficult things and accomplishing goals is the most beautiful thing of all.

—**MADONNA**, SINGER AND ACTOR

No matter what the competition is, I try to find a goal that day and better that goal.

—**BONNIE BLAIR**, OLYMPIC SPEEDSKATER

For me it's the challenge—the challenge to try to beat myself or do better than I did in the past. I try to keep in mind not what I have accomplished but what I have to try to accomplish in the future.

—**JACKIE JOYNER-KERSEE**, OLYMPIC
HEPTATHLETE AND LONG JUMPER

We always attract into our lives whatever we think about most, believe in most strongly, expect on the deepest level, and imagine most vividly.

—SHAKTI GAWAIN, AUTHOR

Nothing's far when one wants to get there.

—QUEEN MARIE OF ROMANIA

Far away in the sunshine are my highest aspirations. I may not reach them, but I can look up and see the beauty, believe in them and try to follow where they lead.

—LOUISA MAY ALCOTT, AUTHOR

Just don't give up trying to do what you really want to do. Where there is love and inspiration, I don't think you can go wrong.

—ELLA FITZGERALD, JAZZ VOCALIST

Yes, I have doubted. I have wandered off the path, but I always return. It is intuitive, an intrinsic, built-in sense of direction. I seem always to find my way home.

—**HELEN HAYES**, ACTOR

You have to know exactly what you want out of your career. If you want to be a star, you don't bother with other things.

—**MARILYN HORNE**, OPERA SIGNER

Before you begin a thing remind yourself that difficulties and delays quite impossible to foresee are ahead. . . . You can only see one thing clearly, and that is your goal. Form a mental vision of that and cling to it through thick and thin.

—**KATHLEEN NORRIS**, ROMANCE NOVELIST

Nothing contributes so much to tranquilize the mind as a steady purpose—a point on which the soul may fix its intellectual eye.

—**MARY WOLLSTONECRAFT**, ENGLISH
WRITER, PHILOSOPHER, AND FEMINIST

I was nervous and confident at the same time, nervous about going out there in front of all of those people, with so much at stake, and confident that I was going to go out there and win.

—**ALTHEA GIBSON**, TENNIS PLAYER

I have always been driven by some distant music—a battle hymn no doubt—for I have been at war from the beginning. I've never looked back before. I've never had the time and it has always seemed so dangerous.

—**BETTE DAVIS**, ACTOR

The one who cares the most wins.

—**ROSEANNE BARR**, ACTOR AND COMEDIAN

We couldn't possibly know where it would lead, but we knew it had to be done.

—**BETTY FRIEDAN**, FEMINIST, ACTIVIST, AND WRITER

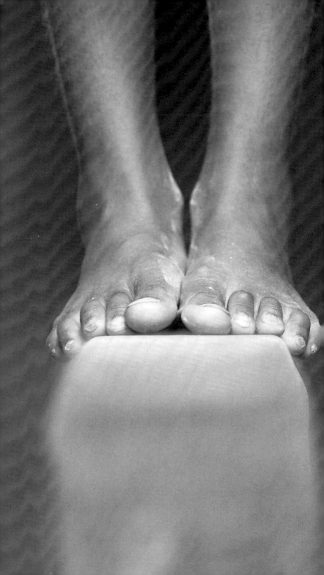

Chapter 17

TRUSTING YOURSELF

Sometimes it seems like other people are always trying to tell you what to do and how to do it. There's so much peer pressure to fit in, to look and act a certain way, and to do what's "cool," that sometimes you can feel like a total loser for even *wanting* to do something that your friends and family don't. The easiest time to lose faith in yourself is when you share your dreams with someone, only to have them say, "Well, *that's* a really dumb idea."

Rather than get mad or discouraged when someone questions your ideas, try to find out *why* they don't support you. They may have some knowledge or experience that you lack, which you might be able to use to refine your idea into an even better one.

More often, you'll find that they *don't* have a good reason for questioning you. It may just be that they have put less thought into the idea than you have, and so they can't really see how it could work. Those are the times when you just have to follow that little inner voice in your head. Although you need to take other people's knowledge and experience into account, any decision you make in this life is *your* decision. When the world doesn't seem to provide any guidance, that's when you need to trust your vision and just *do it!* ✿

The door that nobody else will go in at, seems always to swing open widely for me.

—CLARA BARTON, PIONEERING TEACHER, NURSE, AND HUMANITARIAN

I don't go by the rule book—I lead from the heart, not the head.

—DIANA, PRINCESS OF WALES

Decisions, particularly important ones, have always made me sleepy, perhaps because I know that I will have to make them by instinct, and thinking things out is only what other people tell me I should do.

—LILLIAN HELLMAN, PLAYWRIGHT

Go ahead and do it. It's much easier to apologize after something's been done than to get permission ahead of time.

—GRACE MURRAY HOPPER, COMPUTER SCIENTIST AND U.S. NAVY OFFICER

Instinct is the nose of the mind.

—DELPHINE DE GIRARDIN, FRENCH AUTHOR

I'm not going to limit myself just because some people won't accept the fact that I can do something else.

—**DOLLY PARTON**, COUNTRY MUSIC ARTIST
   AND ACTOR

Criticism . . . makes very little dent upon me, unless I think there is some real justification and something should be done.

—**ELEANOR ROOSEVELT**, FORMER FIRST LADY
   AND CIVIL RIGHTS ACTIVIST

I was the kind nobody thought could make it. I had a funny Boston accent. I couldn't pronounce my R's. I wasn't a beauty.

—**BARBARA WALTERS**, JOURNALIST

I feel there are two people inside of me—me and my intuition. If I go against her, she'll screw me every time, and if I follow her, we get along quite nicely.

—**KIM BASINGER**, ACTOR AND ANIMAL
   RIGHTS ACTIVIST

You must train your intuition—you must trust the small voice inside you which tells you exactly what to say, what to decide.

    —INGRID BERGMAN, ACTOR

Every advance in social progress removes us more and more from the guidance of instinct, obliging us to depend upon reason for the assurance that our habits are really agreeable to the laws of health.

    —EMILY BLACKWELL, ONE OF THE FIRST U.S. WOMEN TO EARN A MEDICAL DEGREE

Every human being has, like Socrates, an attendant spirit; and wise are they who obey its signals. If it does not always tell us what to do, it always cautions us what not to do.

    —LYDIA MARIA CHILD, RIGHTS ACTIVIST, NOVELIST, AND JOURNALIST

Every time you don't follow your inner guidance, you feel a loss of energy, loss of power, a sense of spiritual deadness.

    —SHAKTI GAWAIN, AUTHOR

I move on feeling and have learned to distrust those who don't.

—NIKKI GIOVANNI, POET

Advice is what we ask for when we already know the answer but wish we didn't.

—ERICA JONG, AUTHOR AND EDUCATOR

Doubt yourself and you doubt everything you see. Judge yourself and you see judges everywhere. But if you listen to the sound of your own voice, you can rise above doubt and judgment. And you can see forever.

—NANCY KERRIGAN, OLYMPIC FIGURE
    SKATER

I give myself, sometimes, admirable advice, but I am incapable of taking it.

—LADY MARY WORTLEY MONTAGU,
    ENGLISH WRITER

I'm often wrong, but never in doubt.

—IVY BAKER PRIEST, POLITICIAN

I go by instinct. . . . I don't worry about experience.

 —**BARBRA STREISAND,** SINGER AND ACTOR

Trust your gut.

 —**BARBARA WALTERS,** JOURNALIST

Follow your instincts. That's where true wisdom manifests itself.

 —**OPRAH WINFREY,** TALK SHOW HOST AND
  MEDIA MOGUL

There is only one history of any importance, and it is the history of what you once believed in, and the history of what you came to believe in.

 —**KAY BOYLE,** WRITER, EDUCATOR, AND
  POLITICAL ACTIVIST

What one decides to do in crisis depends on one's philosophy of life, and that philosophy cannot be changed by an incident. If one hasn't any philosophy in crises, others make the decision.

 —**JEANNETTE RANKIN,** FIRST FEMALE
  MEMBER OF THE U.S. CONGRESS

Chapter 18

RESPECTING OTHERS

Think about your three closest friends. Are they all exactly alike? Probably not! Odds are, one of them is a total crack-up, another is really serious, and the third one is kind of in between. One might be really wild and outgoing, while the other two are more quiet and easygoing. But even though you are all different, you have some shared interests and values that help tie the four of you together as friends.

It's important to respect other people's differences. Girls who like to be the center of attention often hate being left out of decisions. Girls who are shy or indecisive often feel more comfortable playing "follow the leader," letting someone else take the lead. Recognizing each other's strengths and weaknesses is so important when it comes to working together as a group.

Yet, we can't get too carried away in our roles,
either. The indecisive girl needs to be a given a
chance to step forward once in a while. The outgoing girl in the group may resent being the one
who always has to plan and organize everything.
Each of us can sometimes feel like we're being
judged or taken for granted . . . even by the
ones who love and understand us best.

Take a minute to think about those things that
make us all different . . . and think about how
wonderful and interesting those differences are.

Differences can be a strength.

> —**CONDOLEEZZA RICE**, FORMER U.S.
> SECRETARY OF STATE

Mom always tells me to celebrate everyone's uniqueness.

> —**HILARY DUFF**, ACTOR, SINGER, AND
> SONGWRITER

The motto should not be: Forgive one another; rather understand one another.

> —**EMMA GOLDMAN**, POLITICAL ACTIVIST

[Tolerance] is the greatest gift of the mind; it requires the same effort of the brain that it takes to balance oneself on a bicycle.

> —**HELEN KELLER**, THE FIRST DEAFBLIND
> PERSON TO GRADUATE FROM COLLEGE

Truth has never been, can never be, contained in any one creed or system.

> —**MARY AUGUSTA WARD**, ENGLISH NOVELIST

I believe every person has the ability to achieve something important, and with that in mind I regard everyone as special.

—**MARY KAY ASH**, BUSINESSWOMAN AND FOUNDER OF MARY KAY COSMETICS

The fact that we are human beings is infinitely more important than all the peculiarities that distinguish human beings from one another.

—**SIMONE DE BEAUVOIR**, FRENCH AUTHOR AND PHILOSOPHER

The sexes in each species of beings . . . are always true equivalents—equals but not identicals.

—**ANTOINETTE BROWN BLACKWELL**, FIRST FEMALE ORDAINED MINISTER IN THE U.S.

To understand another human being you must gain some insight into the conditions which made him what he is.

—**MARGARET BOURKE-WHITE**, PHOTOJOURNALIST

Like snowflakes, the human pattern is never cast twice. We are uncommonly and marvelously intricate in thought and action.

—**ALICE CHILDRESS**, PLAYWRIGHT AND
AUTHOR

Everyone needs to be valued. Everyone has the potential to give something back.

—**DIANA**, PRINCESS OF WALES

Tyranny and anarchy are alike incompatible with freedom, security, and the enjoyment of opportunity.

—**JEANE KIRKPATRICK**, FIRST FEMALE U.S.
AMBASSADOR TO THE UNITED NATIONS

All sweeping assertions are erroneous.

—**LETITIA ELIZABETH LANDON**, ENGLISH
POET AND NOVELIST

Because you're not what I would have you be, I blind myself to who, in truth, you are.

—**MADELEINE L'ENGLE**, NOVELIST

We cannot safely assume that other people's minds work on the same principles as our own. All too often, others with whom we come in contact do not reason as we reason, or do not value the things we value, or are not interested in what interests us.

—ISABEL BRIGGS MYERS, PSYCHOLOGICAL THEORIST

To have one's individuality completely ignored is like being pushed quite out of life. Like being blown out as one blows out a light.

—EVELYN SCOTT, NOVELIST AND PLAYWRIGHT

It's funny how your initial approach to a person can determine your feelings toward them, no matter what facts develop later on.

—DOROTHY UHNAK, NOVELIST

Nobody really knows Indians who cheat them and treat them badly.

—SARAH WINNEMUCCA, FIRST NATIVE AMERICAN WOMAN TO SECURE A COPYRIGHT

It is no good to think that other people are out to serve our interests.

—**IVY COMPTON-BURNETT**, ENGLISH
    NOVELIST

You can stand tall without standing on someone. You can be a victor without having victims.

—**HARRIET WOODS**, POLITICIAN AND
    ACTIVIST

Chapter 19

WORKING TOGETHER

Think of all the things that would be impossible without teamwork.

To stay together, families need every member in the household to pitch in. To win games, sports teams have to rely on both their offense and defense. To make money, businesses require both leaders and workers to strive for the good of the company. To make beautiful music, symphonies need the strings, the woodwinds, the brass, *and* the percussion sections.

To work in teams, we all have to do a lot of difficult balancing. We have to learn to give as well as to take. We need to stand together, but we also need to praise outstanding individuals on the team. We each need to do our share, but we can't be afraid to ask for help when we need it.

Think about the various groups you belong to—your family, your neighborhood, your faith community, your class at school, or the after-school groups in which you participate. Which groups are the strongest? Which groups would you miss the most if you could no longer be a part of them, and why? Are you doing everything you can to be an effective member of each of these teams? ✿

Leader and followers are both following the invisible leader—the common purpose.

> —**MARY PARKER FOLLETT**, SOCIAL WORKER AND CONSULTANT

Competition is about passion for perfection, and passion for other people who join in this impossible quest.

> —**MARIAH BURTON NELSON**, AUTHOR, PUBLIC SPEAKER, AND FORMER PRO BASKETBALL PLAYER

Alone we can do so little; together we can do so much.

> —**HELEN KELLER**, THE FIRST DEAFBLIND PERSON TO GRADUATE FROM COLLEGE

Happiness is not perfected till it is shared.

> —**JANE PORTER**, ENGLISH NOVELIST

The tourist may complain of other tourists, but he would be lost without them.

> —**AGNES REPPLIER**, ESSAYIST

If enough people think of a thing and work hard enough at it, I guess it's pretty nearly bound to happen, wind and weather permitting.

—**LAURA INGALLS WILDER**, AUTHOR

We must stand together; if we don't, there will be no victory for any one of us.

—**MARY HARRIS JONES**, "MOTHER JONES,"
LABOR AND COMMUNITY ORGANIZER

Sharing is sometimes more demanding than giving.

—**MARY CATHERINE BATESON**, WRITER AND
CULTURAL ANTHROPOLOGIST

I've always believed that one woman's success can only help another woman's success.

—**GLORIA VANDERBILT**, ARTIST AND ACTOR

Unity, not uniformity, must be our aim. We attain unity only through variety. Differences must be integrated, not annihilated, not absorbed.

—**MARY PARKER FOLLETT**, SOCIAL WORKER
AND CONSULTANT

We learn best to listen to our own voices if we are listening at the same time to other women—whose stories, for all our differences, turn out, if we listen well, to be our stories also.

—**BARBARA DEMING,** FEMINIST AND PACIFIST

Unless I am a part of everything I am nothing.

—**PENELOPE LIVELY,** ENGLISH NOVELIST

We all have the same dreams.

—**JOAN DIDION,** ESSAYIST AND NOVELIST

That is always our problem, not how to get control of people, but how all together we can get control of a situation.

—**MARY PARKER FOLLETT,** SOCIAL WORKER
    AND CONSULTANT

The streams which would otherwise diverge to fertil-ize a thousand meadows, must be directed into one deep narrow channel before they can turn a mill.

—**ANNA JAMESON,** ENGLISH ESSAYIST

I always feel the movement is a sort of mosaic. Each of us puts in one little stone, and then you get a grea' mosaic at the end.

—**ALICE PAUL**, SUFFRAGIST

Together we make change.

—**BARBARA MIKULSKI**, U.S. SENATOR

Pears cannot ripen alone. So we ripened together.

—**MERIDEL LE SUEUR**, NOVELIST AND ESSAYIST

When one's own problems are unsolvable and all best efforts are frustrated, it is lifesaving to listen to other people's problems.

—**SUZANNE MASSIE**, CONSULTANT, AUTHOR, AND LECTURER

The only alternative to war is peace and the only road to peace is negotiations.

—**GOLDA MEIR**, FORMER PRIME MINISTER OF ISRAEL

We seldom stop to think how many people's lives are entwined with our own. It is a form of selfishness to imagine that every individual can operate on his own.

—**IVY BAKER PRIEST**, POLITICIAN

I am a member of a team, and I rely on the team, I defer to it and sacrifice for it, because the team, not the individual, is the ultimate champion.

—**MIA HAMM**, SOCCER PLAYER

I never did anything alone. Whatever was accomplished in this country was accomplished collectively.

—**GOLDA MEIR**, FORMER PRIME MINISTER OF ISRAEL

To achieve . . . solutions, a variety of ideas and approaches are needed.

—**SUSAN GERKE**, BUSINESS CONSULTANT AND AUTHOR

Chapter 20

CHALLENGING YOURSELF

It's fun to be really good at something, isn't it? Maybe you're the girl the teacher knows he can always call on in class, when no one else knows the answer. Maybe you're the player who always gets picked first when choosing teams in phys ed. Maybe you always get to do the solos in band or choir performances.

But that fun feeling you get from being good at something can sometimes keep you from trying new things that you may not be as good at. It can suddenly be hard for you to envision doing the things that your friends or classmates are trying. Even in your current activities, you can get a little lazy and tell yourself, "If I'm already the best, why try harder?"

But if you don't push yourself, no one else is likely to do it for you. Today, try to open your-

self up to the possibilities of a new experience. Instead of settling, think of some way you can improve your existing skills. Look for opportunities to grow. Surprise yourself! ✿

Always choose people that are better than you. Always choose people that challenge you and are smarter than you. Always be the student.

—SANDRA BULLOCK, ACTOR

You can never be totally settled as an actor or artist or musician. You have to keep the fire under you, because that's what makes you better.

—REESE WITHERSPOON, ACTOR

As long as we dare to dream and don't get in the way of ourselves, anything is possible—there's truly no end to where our dreams can take us.

—HILARY SWANK, ACTOR

I want to be all that I am capable of becoming.

—KATHERINE MANSFIELD, NEW ZEALAND
–BORN SHORT STORY WRITER

If you do things well, do them better. Be daring, be first, be different, be just.

—ANITA RODDICK, FOUNDER OF THE BODY
SHOP

New things cannot come where there is no room.

—MARLO MORGAN, AUTHOR

I think the key is for women not to set any limits.

—MARTINA NAVRATILOVA, PROFESSIONAL
TENNIS PLAYER

I think, at a child's birth, if a mother could ask a fairy godmother to endow it with the most useful gift, that gift should be curiosity.

—ELEANOR ROOSEVELT, FORMER FIRST LADY
AND CIVIL RIGHTS ACTIVIST

I'll always push the envelope. To me, the ultimate sin in life is to be boring. I don't play it safe.

—CYBILL SHEPHERD, ACTOR

Change is the watchword of progression. When we tire of well-worn ways, we seek for new. This restless craving in the souls of men spurs them to climb, and to seek the mountain view.

—ELLA WHEELER WILCOX, POET

I try and learn something new on every movie I do. I try to better myself from everything, and from everyone on the film and from my characters.

—**DAKOTA FANNING**, ACTOR

To try to be better is to be better.

—**CHARLOTTE CUSHMAN**, STAGE ACTOR

The effect of having other interests beyond the domestic works well. The more one does and sees and feels, the more one is able to do, and the more genuine may be one's own appreciation of fundamental things like home, and love, and understanding companionship.

—**AMELIA EARHART**, FIRST WOMAN TO FLY
        OVER THE ATLANTIC OCEAN

Aerodynamically, the bumblebee shouldn't be able to fly, but the bumblebee doesn't know it so it goes on flying anyway.

—**MARY KAY ASH**, BUSINESSWOMAN AND
        FOUNDER OF MARY KAY COSMETICS

It's not a very big step from contentment to complacency.

> —**SIMONE DE BEAUVOIR**, FRENCH AUTHOR
> AND PHILOSOPHER

The minute you settle for less than you deserve, you get even less than you settled for.

> —**MAUREEN DOWD**, NEWSPAPER COLUMNIST

"Good enough never is" has become the motto of this company.

> —**DEBBI FIELDS**, FOUNDER OF MRS. FIELDS
> COOKIES

One can never consent to creep when one feels an impulse to soar.

> —**HELEN KELLER**, THE FIRST DEAFBLIND
> PERSON TO GRADUATE FROM COLLEGE

If I'd been a housemaid, I'd have been the best in Australia—I couldn't help it. It's got to be perfection for me.

> —**NELLIE MELBA**, AUSTRALIAN OPERA SINGER

I might have been born in a hovel but I am determined to travel with the wind and the stars.

—JACQUELINE COCHRAN, PIONEERING
   AVIATOR

So long as we think dugout canoes are the only possibility—all that is real or can be real—we will never see the ship, we will never feel the free wind blow.

—SONIA JOHNSON, FEMINIST AND WRITER

A lot of young girls have looked to their career paths and have said they'd like to be chief. There's been a change in the limits people see.

—WILMA PEARL MANKILLER, FIRST FEMALE
   CHIEF OF THE CHEROKEE NATION

Our being is subject to all the chances of life. There are so many things we are capable of, that we could be or do. The potentialities are so great that we never, any of us, are more than one-fourth fulfilled.

—KATHERINE ANNE PORTER, WRITER

Chapter 21

ME? A ROLE MODEL?

Being a role model can be a big responsibility.
Here are four important keys to being a better
influence in the lives of other kids:

- **Be truthful.** More than any other
  quality, honesty is the quality that girls
  cherish the most in their friends, family, and mentors.

- **Encourage others to solve their own
  problems.** It's easy to act as if you
  have all the answers, and tempting to
  tell others what to do. But the best role
  models don't control or talk down to
  others. Instead, they encourage and
  empower others to find solutions, and
  to discover their own best qualities.

- **Praise, don't complain.** No one likes to be criticized. Instead of focusing on other kids' faults, point out the things that they do well. You'll make them feel good about themselves, and they'll be more likely to rally behind you when you really need them.

- **Be genuine.** Smiles, compliments, and apologies won't do any good if you don't truly mean them. Never be fakey with anyone . . . especially the people who look up to you and who know you well. ✿

My little sister Stella partly looks up to me. She depends on me and I always try to set a good example for her.

—VANESSA ANNE HUDGENS, ACTOR

"Bart, having never received any words of encouragement myself, I'm not sure how they're supposed to sound. But here goes: I believe in you."

—LISA SIMPSON, CARTOON CHARACTER

That power of belief in another human being is one of the most powerful things in the world.

—HILARY SWANK, ACTOR

Everyone has an invisible sign hanging from their neck saying, "Make me feel important." Never forget this message when working with people.

—MARY KAY ASH, BUSINESSWOMAN AND
    FOUNDER OF MARY KAY COSMETICS

To sing is to love and affirm, to fly and soar, to coast into the hearts of the people who listen, to tell them that life is to live, that love is there, that nothing is a promise, but that beauty exists, and must be hunted for and found.

—JOAN BAEZ, FOLKSINGER AND SONGWRITER

Praise is the only gift for which people are really grateful.

—MARGUERITE, COUNTESS OF BLESSINGTON, IRISH NOVELIST

I've learned something from every person on my movies and I learned from [Brittany Murphy] how good it makes other people feel when you're really nice to them. I just want to be more like her.

—DAKOTA FANNING, ACTOR

I praise loudly; I blame softly.

—CATHERINE II, EMPRESS OF RUSSIA

There isn't much that tastes better than praise from those who are wise and capable.

—**SELMA LAGERLÖF**, SWEDISH, FIRST WOMAN TO WIN THE NOBEL PRIZE IN LITERATURE

You take people as far as they will go, not as far as you would like them to go.

—**JEANNETTE RANKIN**, FIRST FEMALE MEMBER OF THE U.S. CONGRESS

To hear how special and wonderful we are is end-lessly enthralling.

—**GAIL SHEEHY**, WRITER AND LECTURER

There is nothing stronger in the world than gentle-ness.

—**HAN SUYIN**, CHINESE-BORN EURASIAN WRITER AND PHYSICIAN

I'm not a competitive person, and I think women like me because they don't think I'm competitive, just nice.

—**BARBARA BUSH**, FORMER FIRST LADY

To feel valued, to know, even if only once in a while, that you can do a job well is an absolutely marvelous feeling.

—**BARBARA WALTERS**, JOURNALIST

The true secret of giving advice is, after you have honestly given it, to be perfectly indifferent whether it is taken or not and never persist in trying to set people right.

—**HANNAH WHITALL SMITH**, SPEAKER AND AUTHOR

When we are listened to, it creates us, makes us unfold and expand. Ideas actually begin to grow within us and come to life.

—**BRENDA UELAND**, JOURNALIST AND AUTHOR

Nobody likes having salt rubbed into their wounds, even if it is the salt of the earth.

—**REBECCA WEST**, ENGLISH-IRISH SUFFRAGIST AND WRITER

Charm is always genuine; it may be superficial but it isn't fake.

—P. D. JAMES, ENGLISH MYSTERY NOVELIST

I really do believe I can accomplish a great deal with a big grin. I know some people find that disconcerting, but that doesn't matter.

—BEVERLY SILLS, OPERA SINGER

Kind words can be short and easy to speak, but their echoes are truly endless.

—MOTHER TERESA, ALBANIAN MISSIONARY
AND HUMANITARIAN

Charm is the ability to make someone else think that both of you are pretty wonderful.

—KATHLEEN WINSOR, NOVELIST

The mode of delivering a truth makes, for the most part, as much impression on the mind of the listener as the truth itself.

—FRANCES WRIGHT, SCOTTISH-BORN
RIGHTS ACTIVIST

Chapter 22

WHEN OPPORTUNITY KNOCKS

Every day brings another chance to take your life in a new direction. But if you don't keep an eye out for those opportunities and take advantage of them when you see them, they may just pass you by.

The secret is to "live in the present, but look to the future." For your first part-time job, it might seem exciting to work at a cool clothing store at the mall. But if you dream of being a journalist someday, taking an unpaid internship at the city newspaper would look much more impressive on your future résumé.

If you dream of going to college someday, maintaining your grades is one of the best ways to increase your chances of winning a scholarship. But many scholarships go to girls who are active

in organizations in and outside school. Joining the debate team might seem like it could get in the way of your studies, but you'll feel different on awards day when you're a high school senior.

Think about the things you'd like to accomplish in the next year or two (or five, or ten). Is there anything you can do today that might make it easier to reach those dreams? ✿

Opportunities are usually disguised as hard work, so most people don't recognize them.

—**ANN LANDERS**, ADVICE COLUMNIST

It is never too late to be what you might have been.

—**GEORGE ELIOT**, PEN NAME OF ENGLISH NOVELIST MARY ANN EVANS

One's feelings waste themselves in words; they ought all to be distilled into action . . . which brings results.

—**FLORENCE NIGHTINGALE**, ENGLISH PIONEER OF MODERN NURSING

When you make a world tolerable for yourself, you make a world tolerable for others.

—**ANAÏS NIN**, CUBAN-FRENCH AUTHOR

What you don't do can be a destructive force.

—**ELEANOR ROOSEVELT**, FORMER FIRST LADY AND CIVIL RIGHTS ACTIVIST

You don't need endless time and perfect conditions. Do it now. Do it today. Do it for twenty minutes and watch your heart start beating.

—**BARBARA SHER**, CAREER AND LIFESTYLE COACH

You may be disappointed if you fail, but you are doomed if you don't try.

—**BEVERLY SILLS**, OPERA SINGER

Commitment leads to action. Action brings your dream closer.

—**MARCIA WIEDER**, DREAM COACH

All you have to do is look straight and see the road, and when you see it, don't sit looking at it—walk.

—**AYN RAND**, NOVELIST AND PHILOSOPHER

You can't build a reputation on what you intend to do.

—**LIZ SMITH**, JOURNALIST AND NEWSPAPER COLUMNIST

Luck is a matter of preparation meeting opportunity.

—**OPRAH WINFREY**, TALK SHOW HOST AND MEDIA MOGUL

Learn to drink the cup of life as it comes.

—**AGNES TURNBULL**, WRITER

The most effective way to do it, is to do it.

—**TONI CADE BAMBARA**, AUTHOR, SOCIAL ACTIVIST, AND PROFESSOR

I don't wait for moods. You accomplish nothing if you do that. Your mind must know it has got to get down to earth.

—**PEARL S. BUCK**, AUTHOR

The bitterest tears shed over graves are for words left unsaid and deeds left undone.

—**HARRIET BEECHER STOWE**, AUTHOR AND ABOLITIONIST

And all that you are sorry for is what you haven't done.

> —MARGARET WIDDEMER, POET

Change your life today. Don't gamble on the future, act now, without delay.

> —SIMONE DE BEAUVOIR, FRENCH AUTHOR
> AND PHILOSOPHER

Can anything be sadder than work unfinished? Yes; work never begun.

> —CHRISTINA GEORGINA ROSSETTI,
> ENGLISH POET

"Now" is the operative word. Everything you put in your way is just a method of putting off the hour when you could actually be doing your dream.

> —BARBARA SHER, CAREER AND LIFESTYLE
> COACH

Opportunities are often things you haven't noticed the first time around.

> —CATHERINE DENEUVE, FRENCH ACTOR

Luck is largely a matter of paying attention.

—SUSAN M. DODD

I have always been waiting for something better—
sometimes to see the best I had snatched from me.

—DOROTHY RED MENDENHALL, FIRST
WOMAN TO GRADUATE FROM JOHNS
HOPKINS MEDICAL SCHOOL

You can kill time or kill yourself, it comes to the same
thing in the end.

—ELSA TRIOLET, FRENCH WRITER

He who hesitates is last.

—MAE WEST, ACTOR

Chapter 23

MAKING YOUR OWN LUCK

Have you ever known one of those girls who seems to have been born under a lucky star? Everything goes her way: she always gets picked to be queen or princess at every school festival, she's every teacher's pet, and the boys practically throw themselves at her feet.

How does she always luck out, when on most days, you feel there's a little rain cloud following you around?

Although all of us enjoy some good fortune in our lives, no one is always *lucky*. Believe it or not, there are things you can do to make good fortune fall your way:

- **Expect the best.** If you wake up every morning with a groan, saying, "Today is going to be a bad day," should you really be surprised when that's exactly what ends up happening? Optimistic girls tend to lead happier lives than grumblers and whiners.

- **Take action.** Instead of letting bad luck push you around, try making your own good luck! Smile at people rather than frowning all the time. Volunteer or ask for the things you want, rather than waiting for them to be offered to you.

It's not fortune that makes that one lucky girl seem so happy and successful. Her cheerfulness and her self-discipline are like magnets that attract the things she wants—those same things that *you* want in your life. ✿

Good luck needs no explanation.

—**SHIRLEY TEMPLE BLACK**, ACTOR, DIPLOMAT, AND AMBASSADOR

Faith is not belief. Belief is passive. Faith is active.

—**EDITH HAMILTON**, AUTHOR AND EDUCATOR

Every thought we think is creating our future.

—**LOUISE L. HAY**, AUTHOR

Anyone who has gumption knows what it is, and anyone who hasn't can never know what it is.

—**LUCY MAUD MONTGOMERY**, CANADIAN AUTHOR

Life is like a mirror. Smile at it and it smiles back at you.

—**MILDRED LISETTE NORMAN**, "PEACE PILGRIM," PEACE ACTIVIST

The worst cynicism: a belief in luck.

—**JOYCE CAROL OATES**, AUTHOR

Miracles occur naturally as expressions of love. The real miracle is the love that inspires them. In this sense everything that comes from love is a miracle.

—**MARIANNE WILLIAMSON**, SPIRITUAL
ACTIVIST, AUTHOR, AND LECTURER

There is no such thing as making the miracle happen spontaneously and on the spot. You've got to work.

—**MARTINA ARROYO**, OPERA SINGER

I've never banked on [luck], and I'm afraid of people who do.

—**LUCILLE BALL**, COMEDIAN AND ACTOR

Luck is not chance, it's toil: fortune's expensive smile is earned.

—**EMILY DICKINSON**, POET

You have to learn the rules of the game. And then you have to play better than anyone else.

—**DIANNE FEINSTEIN**, U.S. SENATOR

The one important thing I've learned over the years is the difference between taking one's work seriously and taking one's self seriously. The first is imperative and the second is disastrous.

—MARGOT FONTEYN, ENGLISH BALLET DANCER

I don't believe in luck. We make our good fortune.

—DR. JOYCE BROTHERS, ADVICE COLUMNIST

Some people go through life trying to find out what the world holds for them only to find out too late that it's what they bring to the world that really counts.

—LUCY MAUD MONTGOMERY, CANADIAN AUTHOR

Pennies do not come from heaven—they have to be earned here on earth.

—MARGARET THATCHER, FORMER BRITISH PRIME MINISTER

Foolish indeed are those who trust to fortune.

—**LADY MURASAKI**, JAPANESE POET,
NOVELIST, AND EMPERIAL MAID OF HONOR

Genius is the gold in the mine; talent is the miner
that works and brings it out.

—**MARGUERITE, COUNTESS OF
BLESSINGTON**, IRISH NOVELIST

It is one thing to be gifted and quite another thing to
be worthy of one's own gift.

—**NADIA BOULANGER**, FRENCH COMPOSER
AND CONDUCTOR

I was born lucky, and I have lived lucky. What I had
was used. What I still have is being used. Lucky.

—**KATHARINE HEPBURN**, ACTOR

No one has a right to sit down and feel hopeless.
There's too much work to do.

—**DOROTHY DAY**, JOURNALIST AND SOCIAL
ACTIVIST

Don't wait for your "ship to come in," and feel angry and cheated when it doesn't. Get going with something small.

—**DR. IRENE KASSORLA**, PSYCHOLOGIST, LECTURER, AND AUTHOR

Don't sit down and wait for the opportunities to come; you have to get up and make them.

—**MADAM C. J. WALKER**, FIRST SELF-MADE FEMALE MILLIONAIRE

Inspiration never arrived when you were searching for it.

—**LISA ALTHER**, AUTHOR

This world is run with far too tight a rein for luck to interfere. Fortune sells her wares; she never gives them. In some form or other, we pay for her favors; or we go empty away.

—**AMELIA BARR**, ENGLISH-AMERICAN NOVELIST

Chapter 24

WORKING HARD

The great inventor Thomas Edison once said, "Genius is 1% inspiration and 99% perspiration."

What does this mean, exactly? It means that being smart and full of great ideas isn't going to be enough to get you ahead in life. In the end, it's more a matter of how you *apply* your intelligence and *how hard you work* at making your dreams come true.

The only way to fully understand the importance of hard work is to apply it to your life. If you're a naturally gifted student who can get straight A's without even trying, you may have to explore something outside academics to see what a difference hard work can make. A part-time job—especially door-to-door sales or something else that pays you commissions (so

that the harder you work, the more money you make)—might be a good place to start.

But if you're struggling in school or in some other aspect of your life, a part-time job may be too much of a distraction. You might instead decide to double the number of hours you spend on things like homework, practicing a musical instrument, training for sports, or any other area in your life that needs a little more "elbow grease." ✿

With education and hard work, it really does not matter where you came from; it matters only where you are going.

—**CONDOLEEZZA RICE**, FORMER U.S. SECRETARY OF STATE

The biggest gift I've ever been given in my life was when my mom said to me, "You can do anything you want as long as you work hard enough."

—**HILARY SWANK**, ACTOR

Success for me isn't a destination, it's a journey. Everybody's working to get to the top but where is the top? It's all about working harder and getting better and moving up and up.

—**RIHANNA**, BARBADIAN SINGER

If your dream is a big dream, and if you want your life to work on the high level that you say you do, there's no way around doing the work it takes to get you there.

—**JOYCE CHAPMAN**, DREAM COACH AND AUTHOR

Hard work has made it easy. That is my secret. That is why I win.

—**NADIA COMANECI**, ROMANIAN GYMNAST

Success comes with hard work—it won't be handed to you.

—**ASHLEY TISDALE**, ACTOR

The only thing that separates successful people from the ones who aren't is the willingness to work very, very hard.

—**HELEN GURLEY BROWN**, AUTHOR, PUBLISHER, AND BUSINESSWOMAN

Success depends in a very large measure upon individual initiative and exertion, and cannot be achieved except by a dint of hard work.

—**ANNA PAVLOVA**, RUSSIAN BALLET DANCER

Nobody ever drowned in his own sweat.

—**ANN LANDERS**, ADVICE COLUMNIST

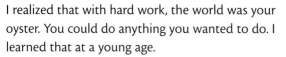

I realized that with hard work, the world was your oyster. You could do anything you wanted to do. I learned that at a young age.

—**CHRIS EVERT**, PROFESSIONAL TENNIS PLAYER

There are no shortcuts to any place worth going.

—**BEVERLY SILLS**, OPERA SINGER

In the spring, at the end of the day, you should smell like dirt.

—**MARGARET ATWOOD**, CANADIAN POET, NOVELIST, AND LITERARY CRITIC

If you want something done, ask a busy person to do it. The more things you do, the more you can do.

—**LUCILLE BALL**, COMEDIAN AND ACTOR

Energy is the power that drives every human being. It is not lost by exertion but maintained by it, for it is a faculty of the psyche.

—**GERMAINE GREER**, AUSTRALIAN WRITER, JOURNALIST, AND FEMINIST

It is not hard work that is dreary; it is superficial work.

— **EDITH HAMILTON**, WRITER AND EDUCATOR

A job is not a career. I think I started out with a job. It turned into a career and changed my life.

— **BARBARA WALTERS**, JOURNALIST

The only genius that's worth anything is the genius for hard work.

— **KATHLEEN WINSOR**, NOVELIST

Work, alternated with needful rest, is the salvation of man or woman.

— **ANTOINETTE BROWN BLACKWELL**, FIRST FEMALE ORDAINED MINISTER IN THE U.S.

I believe in hard work. It keeps the wrinkles out of the mind and spirit.

— **HELENA RUBINSTEIN**, COSMETICS TYCOON

We fought hard. We gave it our best. We did what was right and we made a difference.

—**GERALDINE FERRARO**, FIRST FEMALE U.S. VICE PRESIDENTIAL CANDIDATE

People should tell their children what life is all about—it's about work.

—**LAUREN BACALL**, ACTOR

You've got to sing like you don't need the money. You've got to love like you'll never get hurt. You've got to dance like there's nobody watching. You've got to come from the heart, if you want it to work.

—**SUSANNA CLARK**, SONGWRITER

The only way to enjoy anything in this life is to earn it first.

—**GINGER ROGERS**, ACTOR, DANCER, AND SINGER

A person who has not done one half his day's work by ten o' clock, runs a chance of leaving the other half undone.

—**EMILY BRONTË**, ENGLISH NOVELIST AND POET

There is clearly much left to be done, and whatever else we are going to do, we had better get on with it.

—**ROSALYNN CARTER**, FORMER FIRST LADY

Busy people are never busybodies.

—**ETHEL WATTS MUMFORD**, AUTHOR

Look at a day when you are supremely satisfied at the end. It's not a day when you lounge around doing nothing; it's when you've had everything to do, and you've done it.

—**MARGARET THATCHER**, FORMER BRITISH PRIME MINISTER

I don't think that work ever really destroyed anybody. I think that lack of work destroys them a lot more.

—**KATHARINE HEPBURN**, ACTOR

I am fierce for work. Without work I am nothing.

—**WINIFRED HOLTBY**, ENGLISH NOVELIST
AND JOURNALIST

For the last third of life there remains only work. It alone is always stimulating, rejuvenating, exciting and satisfying.

—**KÄTHE KOLLWITZ**, GERMAN PAINTER,
PRINTMAKER, AND SCULPTOR

Study as if you were going to live forever; live as if you were going to die tomorrow.

—**MARIA MITCHELL**, ASTRONOMER

Chapter 25

STICKING WITH IT

Have you ever tried something new—like a hobby, an artistic activity, or even a video game—only to get frustrated and quit when you saw how much better someone else was at it than you were?

Comparing yourself to other people is not a good way to live your life. No matter how good you are at something, there will always be other people who are better at it than you are. So if you constantly compare yourself to these people, you'll end up feeling like a loser sooner or later. You'll spend years taking up hobbies and interests, only to quickly abandon them after getting discouraged by your slow progress, or by how quickly someone else masters them. Worse yet, you may never even *try* a lot of things— including things that you might end up being really good at!

To succeed at anything, you have to keep working at it. The key is to set your own goals for improvement, and not worry about how you're doing in comparison to your friends, classmates, siblings, or whoever. Ask yourself "How am I doing this activity right now . . . and what would I like to be doing with it in the future?"

Don't set a timeline for yourself . . . it's not a race! Just practice a little every day or every week until you reach your goal. In the end, you'll realize the wisdom in that old saying, "Persistence pays." ⚙

Give it 110% and don't give up!

    —**VANESSA ANNE HUDGENS**, ACTOR

Stay up and really burn the midnight oil. There are no compromises.

    —**LEONTYNE PRICE**, OPERA SINGER

I could not, at any age, be content to take my place by the fireside and simply look on. Life was meant to be lived. Curiosity must be kept alive. One must never, for whatever reason, turn his back on life.

    —**ELEANOR ROOSEVELT**, FORMER FIRST LADY
      AND CIVIL RIGHTS ACTIVIST

When you get into a tight place and everything goes against you, till it seems as though you could not hang on a minute longer, never give up then, for that is just the place and time that the tide will turn.

    —**HARRIET BEECHER STOWE**, AUTHOR AND
      ABOLITIONIST

Keep breathing.

    —**SOPHIE TUCKER**, SINGER AND COMEDIAN

You may have to fight a battle more than once to win it.

—MARGARET THATCHER, FORMER BRITISH
PRIME MINISTER

Our way is not soft grass, it's a mountain path with lots of rocks. But it goes upwards, forward, toward the sun.

—DR. RUTH WESTHEIMER, THERAPIST AND
AUTHOR

There is no point at which you can say, "Well, I'm successful now. I might as well take a nap."

—CARRIE FISHER, ACTOR, SCREENWRITER,
AND NOVELIST

Every great work, every big accomplishment, has been brought into manifestation through holding to the vision, and often just before the big achievement, comes apparent failure and discouragement.

—FLORENCE SCOVEL SHINN, AUTHOR AND
MYSTIC

I try. I am trying. I was trying. I will try. I shall in the meantime try. I sometimes have tried. I shall still by that time be trying.

—**DIANE GLANCY**, POET, AUTHOR, AND
PLAYWRIGHT

When you put your hand to the plow, you can't put it down until you get to the end of the row.

—**ALICE PAUL**, SUFFRAGIST

I wrote for twelve years and collected 250 rejection slips before getting any fiction published, so I guess outside reinforcement isn't all that important to me.

—**LISA ALTHER**, AUTHOR

Perseverance is failing nineteen times and succeeding the twentieth.

—**JULIE ANDREWS**, ACTOR, SINGER, AND
AUTHOR

It's not worthy of human beings to give up.

—**ALVA REIMER MYRDAL**, SWEDISH
DIPLOMAT, POLITICIAN, AND WRITER

It takes far less courage to kill yourself than it takes to make yourself wake up one more time.

—**JUDITH ROSSNER**, NOVELIST

The secret to mountain biking is pretty simple. The slower you go the more likely it is you'll crash.

—**JULI FURTADO**, MOUNTAIN BIKER

There is something in me—I just can't stand to admit defeat.

—**BEVERLY SILLS**, OPERA SINGER

There was no such thing as defeat if you didn't accept it.

—**FAY WELDON**, ENGLISH AUTHOR

To be somebody you must last.

—**RUTH GORDON**, ACTOR AND WRITER

As long as one keeps searching, the answers come.

—**JOAN BAEZ**, FOLKSINGER AND SONGWRITER

We can do anything we want to do if we stick to it long enough.

—**HELEN KELLER**, THE FIRST DEAFBLIND
    PERSON TO GRADUATE FROM COLLEGE

If you don't quit, and don't cheat, and don't run home when trouble arrives, you can only win.

—**SHELLEY LONG**, ACTOR

Part of being a champ is acting like a champ. You have to learn how to win and not run away when you lose. Everyone has bad stretches and real successes.

—**NANCY KERRIGAN**, OLYMPIC FIGURE
    SKATER

People with good intentions never give up!

—**JANE SMILEY**, NOVELIST

The great thing, and the hard thing, is to stick to things when you have outlived the first interest, and not yet got the second, which comes with a sort of mastery.

—**JANET ERSKINE STUART**, EDUCATOR

Chapter 26

OOPS!

Have you ever made a really dumb mistake? If so, did you own up to it? Or did you instead try to cover it up . . . or worse yet, blame it on someone else?

It's important to know that it's totally OK to make mistakes. These days, there is so much pressure to be perfect that most girls go out of their way to avoid screwing up. But their fear of failure—combined with the fact that they're almost guaranteed to run into disappointment when trying new or challenging things—explains why many of them give up on their dreams: they're not prepared for setbacks they'll face in the big journey called "growing up."

Here are the six most important things to remember when it comes to goof-ups:

1. It's a *good* thing to put yourself in challenging situations where you can make mistakes.

2. Once you make a mistake, be brave enough to admit it.

3. Think about what led up to the mistake. Is there something else you could have done to prevent it, but you chose not to?

4. Make a list of things you can do to avoid making the mistake again.

5. Get to the point where you can make fun of your own mistakes (and not get mad at others who might tease you about them).

6. Don't stress out about the mistakes you might make tomorrow: things rarely turn out as bad you fear. And even if they do, you can learn from those mistakes, too! ✿

Do not be afraid of mistakes, providing you do not make the same one twice.

—**ELEANOR ROOSEVELT**, FORMER FIRST LADY
AND CIVIL RIGHTS ACTIVIST

Life is not life unless you make mistakes.

—**JOAN COLLINS**, ENGLISH ACTOR AND
AUTHOR

When you take a big digger [fall] and walk away from it, it can give you more confidence than anything else in the world.

—**PICABO STREET**, DOWNHILL SKIER AND
OLYMPIC GOLD MEDAL WINNER

Mistakes are part of the dues one pays for a full life.

—**SOPHIA LOREN**, ITALIAN ACTOR

Flops are a part of life's menu and I've never been a girl to miss out on any of the courses.

—**ROSALIND RUSSELL**, ACTOR

Sometimes what you want to do has to fail so you won't.

—MARGUERITTE HARMON BRO, NOVELIST

I think success has no rules, but you can learn a great deal from failure.

—JEAN KERR, AUTHOR AND PLAYWRIGHT

There are no mistakes, no coincidences. All events are blessings given to us to learn from.

—ELISABETH KÜBLER-ROSS, SWISS-BORN PSYCHOLOGIST AND AUTHOR

We will be victorious if we have not forgotten how to learn.

—ROSA LUXEMBURG, POLISH-BORN GERMAN SOCIAL PHILOSOPHER

It is very easy to forgive others their mistakes. It takes more grit and gumption to forgive them for having witnessed your own.

—JESSAMYN WEST, WRITER

People fail forward to success.

> —**MARY KAY ASH**, BUSINESSWOMAN AND
> FOUNDER OF MARY KAY COSMETICS

Apparent failure may hold in its rough shell the germs of a success that will blossom in time, and bear fruit throughout eternity.

> —**FRANCES ELLEN WATKINS HARPER**,
> ABOLITIONIST AND POET

If you have made mistakes, even serious mistakes, there is always another chance for you.

> —**MARY PICKFORD**, ACTOR AND MOVIE
> PRODUCER

A series of failures may culminate in the best possible result.

> —**GISELA RICHTER**, ARCHAEOLOGIST AND
> ART HISTORIAN

The sight of a cage is only frightening to the bird that has once been caught.

> —**RACHEL FIELD**, NOVELIST

Experience is how life catches up with us and teaches us to love and forgive each other.

—**JUDY COLLINS**, FOLKSINGER AND SONGWRITER

Failure is just another way to learn how to do something right.

—**MARIAN WRIGHT EDELMAN**, CIVIL RIGHTS AND CHILDREN'S RIGHTS ACTIVIST

The person interested in success has to learn to view failure as a healthy, inevitable part of the process of getting to the top.

—**DR. JOYCE BROTHERS**, ADVICE COLUMNIST

Failure after long perseverance is much grander than never to have a striving good enough to be called a failure.

—**GEORGE ELIOT**, PEN NAME OF ENGLISH NOVELIST MARY ANN EVANS

Keep trying. Take care of the small circle around you. When you have succeeded with them, then move outwards, one small step at a time.

—**AUDREY HEPBURN,** ACTOR AND
HUMANITARIAN

It takes as much courage to have tried and failed as it does to have tried and succeeded.

—**ANNE MORROW LINDBERGH,** AVIATOR
AND WRITER

It is better to be young in your failures than old in your successes.

—**FLANNERY O'CONNOR,** AUTHOR

I had already learned from more than a decade of political life that I was going to be criticized no matter what I did, so I might as well be criticized for something I wanted to do.

—**ROSALYNN CARTER,** FORMER FIRST LADY

Fear nothing, for every renewed effort raises all former failures into lessons, all sins into experience.

—**KATHERINE TINGLEY**, SOCIAL WORKER AND SPIRITUAL PHILOSOPHER

Life is the only real counselor. Wisdom unfiltered through personal experience does not become a part of the moral tissue.

—**EDITH WHARTON**, WRITER AND DESIGNER

When we begin to take our failures nonseriously, it means we are ceasing to be afraid of them. It is of immense importance to learn to laugh at ourselves.

—**KATHERINE MANSFIELD**, NEW ZEALAND–BORN SHORT STORY WRITER

There is a way to look at the past. Don't hide from it. It will not catch you if you don't repeat it.

—**PEARL BAILEY**, SINGER AND ACTOR

Better a false belief than no belief at all.

—**GEORGE ELIOT**, PEN NAME OF ENGLISH NOVELIST MARY ANN EVANS

Supposing you have tried and failed again and again. You may have a fresh start any moment you choose, for this thing that we call "failure" is not the falling down, but the staying down.

> —**MARY PICKFORD**, ACTOR AND MOVIE PRODUCER

Memories are the key not to the past, but to the future.

> —**CORRIE TEN BOOM**, DUTCH AUTHOR AND HOLOCAUST SURVIVOR

To look backward for a while is to refresh the eye, to restore it, and to render it more fit for its prime function of looking forward.

> —**MARGARET FAIRLESS BARBER**, ENGLISH AUTHOR

A mistake is simply another way of doing things.

> —**KATHARINE GRAHAM**, NEWSPAPER PUBLISHER

Chapter 27

STRESS AND ANXIETY

It's natural to get a little stressed or freaked out about some things. Important exams at school, speaking or performing in public, visiting a faraway place for the first time, going out on a first date—just about any girl can get that weird, "butterflies in the stomach" feeling when she or someone she cares about is under pressure, in the spotlight, or encountering something new.

A little bit of anxiety can be a good thing: it can help you be more alert and focused in situations that involve performance or require lots of attention.

But if you get stressed out too often, or too severely, you may suffer from obsessions, phobias, or panic attacks—anxiety that is so bad it keeps you from living a normal life. Too much anxiety might make you feel physically ill, afraid

to go to school, or uninterested in meeting new people or trying new things. You spend most of your days feeling like something truly horrible is going to happen to you or someone you love.

If your anxiety is severe, talk to the school nurse or another trusted adult. They may be able to help you get back to the normal way you once felt.

But if you're just a little nervous about a big event in your life, consider these words from brave women from around the world. ✿

Of course I realized there was a measure of danger. Obviously I faced the possibility of not returning when I first considered going. Once faced and settled there really wasn't any good reason to refer to it again.

—**AMELIA EARHART,** FIRST WOMAN TO FLY
OVER THE ATLANTIC OCEAN

Most people go through life dreading they'll have a traumatic experience.

—**DIANE ARBUS,** PHOTOGRAPHER

When fear seizes, change what you are doing. You are doing something wrong.

—**JEAN CRAIGHEAD GEORGE,** AUTHOR

You will find a joy in overcoming obstacles.

—**HELEN KELLER,** THE FIRST DEAFBLIND
PERSON TO GRADUATE FROM COLLEGE

When you learn not to want things so badly, life comes to you.

—**JESSICA LANGE,** ACTOR

Everybody knows if you are too careful you are so occupied in being careful that you are sure to stumble over something.

—**GERTRUDE STEIN**, WRITER

Events that are predestined require but little management. They manage themselves. They slip into place while we sleep, and suddenly we are aware that the thing we fear to attempt, is already accomplished.

—**AMELIA BARR**, ENGLISH-AMERICAN
NOVELIST

If it is your time, love will track you down like a cruise missile.

—**LYNDA BARRY**, CARTOONIST AND AUTHOR

Great self-destruction follows upon unfounded fear.

—**URSULA K. LE GUIN**, AUTHOR

You just have to learn not to care about the dust mites under the beds.

—**MARGARET MEAD**, ANTHROPOLOGIST

Stress is basically a disconnection from the earth, a forgetting of the breath. Stress is an ignorant state. It believes that everything is an emergency. Nothing is that important. Just lie down.

—NATALIE GOLDBERG, AUTHOR AND
    TEACHER

Worry a little bit every day and in a lifetime you will lose a couple of years. If something is wrong, fix it if you can. But train yourself not to worry. Worry never fixes anything.

—MARY HEMINGWAY, JOURNALIST

You can't start worrying about what's going to happen. You get spastic enough worrying about what's happening now.

—LAUREN BACALL, ACTOR

If things happen all the time you are never nervous. It is when they are not happening that you are nervous.

—GERTRUDE STEIN, WRITER

Worry is like a rocking chair—it keeps you moving but doesn't get you anywhere.

—**CORRIE TEN BOOM**, DUTCH AUTHOR AND HOLOCAUST SURVIVOR

Death does not frighten me, but dying obscurely and above all uselessly does.

—**ISABELLE EBERHARDT**, SWISS-ALGERIAN EXPLORER AND WRITER

A man ninety years old was asked to what he attributed his longevity. "I reckon," he said, with a twinkle in his eye, "it's because most nights I went to bed and slept when I should have sat up and worried."

—**DOROTHEA KENT**, ACTOR

Everyone thought I was bold and fearless and even arrogant, but inside I was always quaking.

—**KATHARINE HEPBURN**, ACTOR

Worry less about what other people think about you, and more about what you think about them.

—**FAY WELDON**, ENGLISH AUTHOR

Mountains appear more lofty the nearer they are approached, but great men resemble them not in this particular.

—MARGUERITE, COUNTESS OF
   BLESSINGTON, IRISH NOVELIST

It is far harder to kill a phantom than a reality.

—VIRGINIA WOOLF, ENGLISH AUTHOR

The really frightening thing about middle age is that you know you'll grow out of it!

—DORIS DAY, SINGER, ACTOR, AND ANIMAL
   WELFARE ACTIVIST

That fear of missing out on things makes you miss out on everything.

—ETTY HILLESUM, DUTCH DIARIST AND
   HOLOCAUST VICTIM

T'ain't worthwhile to wear a day all out before it comes.

—SARAH ORNE JEWETT, NOVELIST AND
   SHORT STORY WRITER

Chapter 28

ENJOYING THE MYSTERY

Have you ever received a surprise e-mail, text message, MySpace comment, Facebook "poke," or postal package? Maybe a birthday greeting from an old friend, or some free product you sent away for (but then forgot about, until it arrived in your mailbox)? You probably couldn't wait to open it so that you could solve the mystery of what was inside. From that day on, checking your mailbox, inbox, or profile page on a social networking Web site probably always involved a little bit of anticipation—you couldn't help but wonder what sorts of surprises were in there, waiting for you.

Imagine how fun things would be if you treated every *day* as if it were an inbox—full of mysteries and surprises waiting to be discovered and opened. Sure, some days your life's inbox will be disappointingly empty. Or the only surprises

you find there will be for other people. But the *possibility* of learning something new or reconnecting with a friend always keeps you coming back.

Greeting your day that way is sure a lot better than dreading the unforeseen things the day might bring. Although you'll still have to deal with life's equivalent of annoying spam or junk mail (like maybe surprise quizzes at school, or hearing that there's a mean rumor going around about you), you'll be open to more solutions and possibilities, too. ✿

It's quite possible to leave your home for a walk in the early morning air and return a different person—beguiled, enchanted.

—**MARY ELLEN CHASE**, NOVELIST

Life is not orderly. No matter how we try to make life so, right in the middle of it we die, lose a leg, fall in love, drop a jar of applesauce.

—**NATALIE GOLDBERG**, AUTHOR AND
TEACHER

Time has told me less than I need to know.

—**GWEN HARWOOD**, POET AND LIBRETTIST

Truly nothing is to be expected but the unexpected.

—**ALICE JAMES**, DIARIST

The only thing that makes life possible is permanent, intolerable uncertainty, not knowing what comes next.

—**URSULA K. LE GUIN**, AUTHOR

Nothing, perhaps, is strange, once you have accepted life itself, the great strange business which includes all lesser strangeness.

—**ROSE MACAULAY,** ENGLISH NOVELIST

None of us knows what the next change is going to be, what unexpected opportunity is just around the corner, waiting a few months or a few years to change all the tenor of our lives.

—**KATHLEEN NORRIS,** ROMANCE NOVELIST

All decisions are made on insufficient evidence.

—**RITA MAE BROWN,** WRITER

The shortest period of time lies between the minute you put some money away for a rainy day and the unexpected arrival of rain.

—**JANE BRYANT QUINN,** JOURNALIST

The power to love what is purely abstract is given to few.

—**MARGOT ASQUITH,** ENGLISH-SCOTTISH
SOCIALITE AND AUTHOR

I wanted a perfect ending. Now I've learned, the hard way, that some poems don't rhyme, and some stories don't have a clear beginning, middle, and end. Life is about not knowing, having to change, taking the moment and making the best of it without knowing what's going to happen next.

—**GILDA RADNER**, COMEDIAN AND ACTOR

Where will I be five years from now? I delight in not knowing.

—**MARLO THOMAS**, ACTOR

We live in an epoch in which the solid ground of our preconceived ideas shakes daily under our certain feet.

—**BARBARA WARD**, ENGLISH ECONOMIST
AND WRITER

Exceptional talent does not always win its reward unless favoured by exceptional circumstances.

—**MARY ELIZABETH BRADDON**, ENGLISH
NOVELIST

Life is my college. May I graduate well, and earn some honors!

—**LOUISA MAY ALCOTT**, AUTHOR

It's a simple formula: do your best and somebody might like it.

—**DOROTHY BAKER**, NOVELIST

There is no security, no assurance that because we wrote something good two months ago, we will do it again. Actually, every time we begin, we wonder how we ever did it before.

—**NATALIE GOLDBERG**, AUTHOR AND TEACHER

For me life is a challenge. And it will be a challenge if I live to be a hundred or if I get to be a trillionaire.

—**BEAH RICHARDS**, ACTOR AND WRITER

Love involves a peculiar unfathomable combination of understanding and misunderstanding.

—**DIANE ARBUS**, PHOTOGRAPHER

Real love is a pilgrimage. It happens when there is no strategy, but it is very rare because most people are strategists.

—**ANITA BROOKNER**, ENGLISH NOVELIST
AND ART HISTORIAN

Accept that all of us can be hurt, that all of us can—and surely will at times—fail. Other vulnerabilities, like being embarrassed or risking love, can be terrifying, too.

—**DR. JOYCE BROTHERS**, ADVICE COLUMNIST

Every time I think that I'm getting old, and gradually going to the grave, something else happens.

—**LILLIAN CARTER**, PEACE CORPS
VOLUNTEER AND MOTHER OF FORMER
PRESIDENT JIMMY CARTER

The pain of love is the pain of being alive. It is a perpetual wound.

—**MAUREEN DUFFY**, WRITER

There is no way to take the danger out of human relationships.

—BARBARA GRIZZUTI HARRISON,
JOURNALIST, ESSAYIST, AND MEMOIRIST

When something has been perfect, there is a tendency to try hard to repeat it.

—EDNA O'BRIEN, IRISH NOVELIST AND
SHORT STORY WRITER

Impermanence is the very essence of joy—the drop of bitterness that enables one to perceive the sweet.

—MYRTLE REED, AUTHOR

No great deed is done by falterers who ask for certainty.

—GEORGE ELIOT, PEN NAME OF ENGLISH
NOVELIST MARY ANN EVANS

Fluidity and discontinuity are central to the reality in which we live.

—MARY CATHERINE BATESON, WRITER AND
CULTURAL ANTHROPOLOGIST

If we can recognize that change and uncertainty are basic principles, we can greet the future and the transformation we are undergoing with the understanding that we do not know enough to be pessimistic.

—HAZEL HENDERSON, FUTURIST AND ECONOMIST

Isn't it splendid to think of all the things there are to find out about? It just makes me feel glad to be alive—it's such an interesting world. It wouldn't be half so interesting if we knew all about everything, would it? There'd be no scope for imagination then, would there?

—LUCY MAUD MONTGOMERY, CANADIAN AUTHOR

Courage can't see around corners, but goes around them anyway.

—MIGNON MCLAUGHLIN, JOURNALIST AND AUTHOR

Chapter 29

Being Brave

Girls who play varsity football with the boys. Girls you see on TV, climbing Mount Kilimanjaro. Girls who learned to swim—*underwater*—when they were only three or four years old. Are brave girls just *born* that way . . . or are they *made*?

Whether you're already queen of the skateboard park, or just dreaming of what it might be like to backpack across Europe someday, there are things you can do today to supercharge your girl power:

1. **Think positive.** If there's one quality shared by daring girls everywhere, it's an undying belief in themselves. No "doubting Debbie" ever became an astronaut or Olympic sprinter!

2. **Prepare for the challenge.** Whether it's physical adventure or intellectual risk, you need to acquire the skills, training, and other resources the task requires. Some girls may seem like "naturals" when they're out there showing what they're made of. But they probably got that way only after years of preparation and hard work.

3. **Know the difference between real versus imaginary risks.** Many girls think flying in a plane is dangerous, but it's actually the safest form of travel. But even more girls will get on a mountain bike without wearing a helmet . . . and that's just plain dumb!

If you're having trouble finding your inner superhero, just follow the advice of the brave women in this chapter. ✿

Courage is very important. Like a muscle, it is strengthened by use.

—RUTH GORDON, ACTOR AND WRITER

Fear is a sign—usually a sign that I'm doing something right.

—ERICA JONG, AUTHOR AND EDUCATOR

I became more courageous by doing the very things I needed to be courageous for—first, a little, and badly. Then, bit by bit, more and better.

—AUDRE LORDE, WRITER, POET, AND ACTIVIST

A woman's life can really be a succession of lives, each revolving around some emotionally compelling situation or challenge, and each marked off by some intense experience.

—WALLIS SIMPSON, DUCHESS OF WINDSOR

There are some women who seem to be born without fear, just as there are people who are born without the ability to feel pain. . . . Providence appears to protect such women, maybe out of astonishment.

—MARGARET ATWOOD, CANADIAN POET, NOVELIST, AND LITERARY CRITIC

I think laughter may be a form of courage. . . . As humans we sometimes stand tall and look into the sun and laugh, and I think we are never more brave than when we do that.

—LINDA ELLERBEE, JOURNALIST

Grab the broom of anger and drive off the beast of fear.

—ZORA NEALE HURSTON, AUTHOR AND FOLKLORIST

Become so wrapped up in something that you forget to be afraid.

—LADY BIRD JOHNSON, FORMER FIRST LADY

Being "brave" means doing or facing something frightening. . . . Being "fearless" means being without fear.

> —**PENELOPE LEACH**, ENGLISH AUTHOR AND PSYCHOLOGIST

If you are brave too often, people will come to expect it of you.

> —**MIGNON MCLAUGHLIN**, JOURNALIST AND AUTHOR

The best protection any woman can have . . . is courage.

> —**ELIZABETH CADY STANTON**, WOMEN'S RIGHTS ACTIVIST

Human beings need to belong to a tradition and equally need to know about the world in which they find themselves.

> —**PAULA GUNN ALLEN**, NATIVE AMERICAN WRITER AND ACTIVIST

Courage is fear that has said its prayers.

—**DOROTHY BERNARD**, SILENT FILM ACTOR

When life's problems seem overwhelming, look around and see what other people are coping with. You may consider yourself fortunate.

—**ANN LANDERS**, ADVICE COLUMNIST

A champion is afraid of losing. Everyone else is afraid of winning.

—**BILLIE JEAN KING**, PROFESSIONAL TENNIS PLAYER

I am not afraid . . . I was born to do this.

—**JOAN OF ARC**, FRENCH MILITARY LEADER

Every problem in your life goes away in front of a bull because this problem, the bull, is bigger than all other problems. Of course, I have fear, but it is fear that I will fail the responsibility I have taken on in front of all those people—not fear of the bull.

—**CRISTINA SÁNCHEZ**, RETIRED SPANISH BULLFIGHTER

I never wanted to be a hero, but on the other hand I am not anxious to cultivate cowardice.

—GERTRUDE STEIN, WRITER

Real courage is when you know you're licked before you begin, but you begin anyway and see it through no matter what.

—HARPER LEE, PULITZER PRIZE–WINNING AUTHOR

If one is willing to do a thing he is afraid to do, he does not have to . . . face a situation fearlessly, and [if] there is no situation to face; it falls away of its own weight.

—FLORENCE SCOVEL SHINN, AUTHOR AND MYSTIC

Fear is a question: What are you afraid of, and why? Just as the seed of health is an illness, because illness contains information, our fears are a treasure house of self-knowledge if we explore them.

—MARILYN FERGUSON, AUTHOR, MYSTIC, AND SPEAKER

Only when we are no longer afraid do we begin to live.

—**DOROTHY THOMPSON**, JOURNALIST

It takes great courage to break with one's past history and stand alone.

—**MARION WOODMAN**, CANADIAN AUTHOR

How very little can be done under the spirit of fear.

—**FLORENCE NIGHTINGALE**, ENGLISH PIONEER OF MODERN NURSING

Fear is one thing. To let fear grab you and swing you around by the tail is another.

—**KATHERINE PATERSON**, CHILDREN'S BOOK AUTHOR

Talent is helpful in writing, but guts are absolutely necessary.

—**JESSAMYN WEST**, WRITER

I wanted to be scared again. . . . I wanted to feel unsure again. That's the only way I learn, the only way I feel challenged.

—**CONNIE CHUNG**, JOURNALIST

I am never afraid of what I know.

—**ANNA SEWELL**, ENGLISH NOVELIST

Think like a queen. A queen is not afraid to fail. Failure is another steppingstone to greatness.

—**OPRAH WINFREY**, TALK SHOW HOST AND MEDIA MOGUL

Chapter 30

THINGS ARE ALWAYS CHANGING

Life is full of changes. Your body changes a lot, beginning around middle school. Your feelings about dating probably start to change a little, too. Your interests change, your classes change, and usually you'll change schools once or twice. Most of these changes are usually just a little inconvenient. Some can even be exciting!

But some of life's other changes are anything but fun. When parents separate or divorce, when a pet runs away, when a loved one dies, when you can't seem to fit in and find acceptance at school—those transitions are generally really hard.

When it comes to minor interruptions to your daily routine, try not to overreact. Often things will get back to normal before you know it.

Even if they don't, you'd be surprised how quickly you can adjust and forget that change even happened.

For serious losses in your life or your family's, give yourself time to grieve. After these types of changes, many girls may take a year or more before their life begins to feel "normal" again. Maintain close relationships with friends, aunts, teachers, or other people in your support network during this time. You'll go through a lot of emotional ups and downs during the process.

But if change causes you to develop severe depression, anxiety, or phobias, talk to a trusted adult as soon as possible. Those reactions aren't a normal part of coping with loss, and you need to get help with them before they ruin what's left of that great life you still have ahead of you. ⚙

We each have a role that requires us to change and become more responsible for shaping our own future.

—HILLARY RODHAM CLINTON,
SENATOR, FORMER FIRST LADY, AND U.S.
PRESIDENTIAL CANDIDATE

The mind of the most logical thinker goes so easily from one point to another that it is not hard to mistake motion for progress.

—MARGARET COLLIER GRAHAM, AUTHOR

You don't have to be afraid of change. You don't have to worry about what's being taken away. Just look to see what's been added.

—JACKIE GREER, FIRST FEMALE OFFICER OF
A MAJOR U.S. BANK

No one can persuade another to change. Each of us guards a gate of change that can only be opened from the inside. We cannot open the gate of another, either by argument or emotional appeal.

—MARILYN FERGUSON, AUTHOR, MYSTIC,
AND SPEAKER

It's the most unhappy people who most fear change.

—**MIGNON MCLAUGHLIN**, JOURNALIST AND
AUTHOR

Everyday life confronts us with new problems to be
solved which force us to adjust our old programs
accordingly.

—**DR. ANN FARADAY**, DREAM ANALYST

Changes are not only possible and predictable, but
to deny them is to be an accomplice to one's own
unnecessary vegetation.

—**GAIL SHEEHY**, WRITER AND LECTURER

I have found that sitting in a place where you have
never sat before can be inspiring.

—**DODIE SMITH**, ENGLISH NOVELIST AND
PLAYWRIGHT

You must change in order to survive.

—**PEARL BAILEY**, SINGER AND ACTOR

People change and forget to tell each other.

—**LILLIAN HELLMAN**, PLAYWRIGHT

We measure success and depth by length and time, but it is possible to have a deep relationship that doesn't always stay the same.

—**BARBARA HERSHEY**, ACTOR

We're just getting started. We're just beginning to meet what will be the future.

—**GRACE MURRAY HOPPER**, COMPUTER SCIENTIST AND U.S. NAVY OFFICER

Nothing should be permanent except struggle with the dark side within ourselves.

—**SHIRLEY MACLAINE**, ACTOR AND MYSTIC

Things good in themselves . . . perfectly valid in the integrity of their origins, become fetters if they cannot alter.

—**FREYA STARK**, ENGLISH TRAVEL WRITER

I've learned that you'll never be disappointed if you always keep an eye on uncharted territory, where you'll be challenged and growing and having fun.

—**KIRSTIE ALLEY**, ACTOR

Those interested in perpetuating present conditions are always in tears about the marvelous past that is about to disappear, without having so much as a smile for the young future.

—**SIMONE DE BEAUVOIR**, FRENCH AUTHOR
    AND PHILOSOPHER

The most amazing thing about little children . . . was their fantastic adaptability.

—**KRISTIN HUNTER**, WRITER

Let a man turn to his own childhood—no further— if he will renew his sense of remoteness, and of the mystery of change.

—**ALICE MEYNELL**, ENGLISH POET AND
    SUFFRAGIST

It is never any good dwelling on goodbyes. It is not the being together that it prolongs, it is the parting.

—ELIZABETH ASQUITH BIBESCO, ENGLISH WRITER

Someday change will be accepted as life itself.

—SHIRLEY MACLAINE, ACTOR AND MYSTIC

The things we fear most in organizations—fluctuations, disturbances, imbalances—are the primary sources of creativity.

—MARGARET J. WHEATLEY, WRITER AND MANAGEMENT CONSULTANT

Every new truth begins in a shocking heresy.

—MARGARET DELAND, NOVELIST AND POET

Birth is violent, whether it be the birth of a child or the birth of an idea.

—MARIANNE WILLIAMSON, SPIRITUAL ACTIVIST, AUTHOR, AND LECTURER

Chapter 31

MOVING ON AFTER HARD TIMES

It's too easy to lose hope when things don't work out quite the way you had planned.

If you get "dumped" by someone you really care about, you might worry that there's something wrong with you that will keep you from ever finding love or happiness. If you get cut from a cheerleading squad, dance line, or sports team, you may feel like the biggest, no-talent loser ever to walk the face of the planet. It can feel as though you've walked down a really long trail, only to discover that it's a dead end. Where are you supposed to go *now*?

Don't be too obsessed about how "things never go your way." This time of your life is a period when you're *not supposed to be perfect* at everything; it's a time when you should expose your-

self to things that *might or might not* become a part of your life in the years ahead. Some people find their special talents and life partners at a young age, while others try many different things and meet many different people before they discover their true purpose.

Whatever you do, don't turn to alcohol, drugs, or other unhealthy escapes from your frustrations. Find a kindhearted, listening person who truly cares about you, and who can remind of you of all your wonderful qualities and talents. ✿

When something bad happens to me, I think I'm able to deal with it in a pretty good way. That makes me lucky. Some people fall apart at the first little thing that happens.

—CHRISTIE BRINKLEY, MODEL

I have always grown from my problems and challenges, from the things that didn't work out. That's when I've really learned.

—CAROL BURNETT, ACTOR AND COMEDIAN

Suffering raises up those souls that are truly great; it is only small souls that are made mean-spirited by it.

—ALEXANDRA DAVID-NÉEL, BELGIAN
EXPLORER AND WRITER

A wounded deer leaps highest.

—EMILY DICKINSON, POET

It is only the women whose eyes have been washed clear with tears who get the broad vision that makes them little sisters to all the world.

—DOROTHY DIX, JOURNALIST

To live is to suffer, to survive is to find some meaning
in the suffering.

—ROBERTA FLACK, SINGER

I think my biggest achievement is that after going
through a rather difficult time, I consider myself com-
paratively sane. I'm proud of that.

—JACQUELINE KENNEDY ONASSIS, FORMER
FIRST LADY

If you want a place in the sun, you've got to put up
with a few blisters.

—ABIGAIL VAN BUREN, ADVICE COLUMNIST

True knowledge comes only through suffering.

—ELIZABETH BARRETT BROWNING,
ENGLISH POET

Suffering has always been with us, does it really matter in what form it comes? All that matters is how we
bear it and how we fit it into our lives.

—ETTY HILLESUM, DUTCH DIARIST AND
HOLOCAUST VICTIM

And I think that's important, to know how the water's gone over the dam before you start to describe it. It helps to have been over the dam yourself.

—E. ANNIE PROULX, JOURNALIST AND AUTHOR

Flowers grow out of dark moments.

—CORITA KENT, ARTIST AND EDUCATOR

Those who don't know how to weep with their whole heart don't know how to laugh either.

—GOLDA MEIR, FORMER PRIME MINISTER OF ISRAEL

You can't be brave if you've only had wonderful things happen to you.

—MARY TYLER MOORE, ACTOR AND COMEDIAN

Hot water is my native element. I was in it as a baby, and I have never seemed to get out of it ever since.

—DAME EDITH SITWELL, ENGLISH POET AND CRITIC

Everybody's heart is open, you know, when they have recently escaped from severe pain, or are recovering the blessing of health.

—JANE AUSTEN, ENGLISH NOVELIST

Challenges make you discover things about yourself that you never really knew. They're what make the instrument stretch, what make you go beyond the norm.

—CICELY TYSON, ACTOR

When you can't remember why you're hurt, that's when you're healed. When you have to work real hard to re-create the pain, and you can't quite get there, that's when you're better.

—JANE FONDA, ACTOR AND ACTIVIST

If we did not sometimes taste of adversity, prosperity would not be so welcome.

—ANNE BRADSTREET, POET AND FIRST
    WOMAN TO BE PUBLISHED IN COLONIAL
    AMERICA

A major advantage of age is learning to accept people without passing judgment.

> —LIZ CARPENTER, WRITER, FEMINIST, AND PUBLIC SPEAKER

Birds sing after a storm; why shouldn't people feel as free to delight in whatever remains to them?

> —ROSE KENNEDY, MOTHER OF U.S. PRESIDENT JOHN FITZGERALD KENNEDY

Your first big trouble can be a bonanza if you live through it. Get through the first trouble, and you'll probably make it through the next one.

> —RUTH GORDON, ACTOR AND WRITER

Being disabled gave me an immense advantage. People are kinder to you. It puts you on a different level than if you go into a situation whole and secure.

> —DOROTHEA LANGE, PHOTOGRAPHER AND PHOTOJOURNALIST

Chapter 32

TAKING THINGS ONE STEP AT A TIME

If you're like most girls, you'd probably prefer to be anywhere other than where you are right now.

When you're in grade school, you can't wait for the later curfews and increased freedom of being a middle schooler. When you're in middle school, you can't wait until you're in high school and are old enough to drive. When you're in high school, the thought of graduating so that you can be completely done with school (or better yet, be in college) can make you eager for today to pass and for tomorrow to already be here.

Whatever you envision for your future, it's important not to get impatient waiting for it to happen. If you spend your time wishing your

days away, you'll miss out on the wonderful things that today can bring you. More important, the steps you take today are the building blocks with which you create your future.

Take a little time today to stop and smell the roses . . . and enjoy *where* and *who* you are!

Home wasn't built in a day.

> —JANE ACE, RADIO COMEDIAN

You don't just luck into things. . . . You build step by step, whether it's friendships or opportunities.

> —BARBARA BUSH, FORMER FIRST LADY

If we take care of the moments, the years will take care of themselves.

> —MARIA EDGEWORTH, ENGLISH-IRISH
> NOVELIST

There are very few human beings who receive the truth, complete and staggering, by instant illumination. Most of them acquire it fragment by fragment, on a small scale, by successive developments, cellularly, like a laborious mosaic.

> —ANAÏS NIN, CUBAN-FRENCH AUTHOR

Connections are made slowly, sometimes they grow underground.

> —MARGE PIERCY, POET, NOVELIST, AND
> SOCIAL ACTIVIST

Instead of thinking about where you are, think about where you want to be. It takes twenty years of hard work to become an overnight success.

—**DIANA RANKIN**, AUTHOR, MYSTIC, AND SPEAKER

The world doesn't come to the clever folks, it comes to the stubborn, obstinate, one-idea-at-a-time people.

—**MARY ROBERTS RINEHART**, MYSTERY WRITER AND PLAYWRIGHT

Inspiration does not come like a bolt, nor is it kinetic energy striving, but it comes to us slowly and quietly and all the time.

—**BRENDA UELAND**, JOURNALIST AND AUTHOR

The growth of understanding follows an ascending spiral rather than a straight line.

—**JOANNA FIELD**, PEN NAME OF MARION MILNER, ENGLISH PSYCHOANALYST AND AUTHOR

I look at victory as milestones on a very long highway.

—JOAN BENOIT SAMUELSON, FIRST
    WOMEN'S OLYMPIC MARATHON CHAMPION

It's a long old road, but I know I'm gonna find the end.

—BESSIE SMITH, BLUES SINGER

No first step can be really great; it must of necessity possess more of prophecy than of achievement; nevertheless it is by the first step that a man marks the value, not only of his cause, but of himself.

—KATHERINE CECIL THURSTON, IRISH
    NOVELIST

We must not, in trying to think about how we can make a big difference, ignore the small daily differences we can make which, over time, add up to big differences that we often cannot foresee.

—MARIAN WRIGHT EDELMAN, CIVIL RIGHTS
    AND CHILDREN'S RIGHTS ACTIVIST

I am convinced that there are times in everybody's experience when there is so much to be done, that the only way to do it is to sit down and do nothing.

—**FANNY FERN**, COLUMNIST AND CHILDREN'S AUTHOR

See how time makes all grief decay.

—**ADELAIDE PROCTOR**, POET AND SONGWRITER

Cultural transformation announces itself in sputtering fits and starts, sparked here and there by minor incidents, warmed by new ideas that may smolder for decades. In many different places, at different times, the kindling is laid for the real conflagration—the one that will consume the old landmarks and alter the landscape forever.

—**MARILYN FERGUSON**, AUTHOR, MYSTIC, AND SPEAKER

It is not the straining for great things that is most effective; it is the doing the little things, the common duties, a little better and better.

—ELIZABETH STUART PHELPS, NOVELIST

One only gets to the top rung of the ladder by steadily climbing up one at a time, and suddenly all sorts of powers, all sorts of abilities which you thought never belonged to you—suddenly become within your own possibility and you think, "Well, I'll have a go, too."

—MARGARET THATCHER, FORMER BRITISH PRIME MINISTER

I want to be in the Olympics and get a gold medal. I can't wait for that to happen.

—SARAH HUGHES, FIGURE SKATER, AT AGE EIGHT—NINE YEARS BEFORE SHE WON THE GOLD MEDAL AT THE 2002 OLYMPICS

INDEX

INDEX

About the Authors

Steve Deger and Leslie Ann Gibson have served as volunteer speakers, fund-raisers, and "Bigs" for Big Brothers Big Sisters of America. Previous collaborators on *The Book of Positive Quotations* (second edition) and *The Little Book of Positive Quotations*, the husband-and-wife team lives in Minneapolis, Minnesota.